CHOREOGRAPHY

A BASIC APPROACH USING IMPROVISATION

Sandra Cerny Minton, PhD
University of Northern Colorado

Human Kinetics Publishers, Inc.
Champaign, IL

00016525

Library of Congress Cataloging-in-Publication Data

Minton, Sandra C., 1943-
  Choreography: a basic approach using improvisation.

  Bibliography: p.
  Includes index.
  1. Choreography. I. Title.
  GV1782.5.M56   1986   792.8'2   86-10442
  ISBN 0-87322-071-4

Developmental Editor: Sue Wilmoth, PhD
Production Director: Ernest Noa
Copy Editor: Kevin Neely
Typesetter: Theresa Bear
Text Design: Julie Szamocki
Text Layout: Lezli Harris
Printed By: United Graphics
Cover photo courtesy of Bill Scherer

42909

Credits

Illustrations by Ilene Van Gossen, Jackson, Wyoming

Studio photographs by Dr. James Wanner, University of Northern Colorado, Greeley, Colorado

On stage and cover photographs by Bill Scherer/Centennial Photo, Greeley, Colorado (cover photo *All in Time*, choreography Karen Genoff)

ISBN: 0-87322-071-4

Printed in the United States of America

10   9   8   7   6   5   4   3   2

Human Kinetics Publishers, Inc.   *UK Office*:
Box 5076   Human Kinetics Publishers (UK) Ltd.
Champaign, IL 61825-5076   P.O. Box 18
1-800-747-4457   Rawdon, Leeds LS19 6TG
                                         England
                                         (0532) 504211

Dedication

To my parents who made me aware of the value of an education and of having perseverance; and to all the teachers who encouraged my creative projects and ideas.

Contents

Preface

My interest in writing this book is first to share with others the joys of creating in movement and discovering the infinite variety that can be found within the dance art form. Movement is thus viewed as a medium for artistic expression. At the same time, I hope that this book will help the reader to become more aware of the subtleties found in the movements of daily life and to use these new perceptions to enhance creativity in composing dances.

I believe that the basic approach of this book takes some of the mystery out of choreographing, allowing beginners to feel comfortable with movement and the creative process of forming movement into dances. This text is based on my experience in teaching dance composition to beginners for many years. It is intended to enable the reader to avoid some of the problems typically experienced during the initial efforts of the choreographic learning process. A unique aspect of this book is the suggestions it offers for dealing with the more difficult aspects of creative work. Suggestions are also presented for enhancing receptivity to imagery and other ideas of movement that arise during improvisation.

Chapter 1 attempts to give beginning choreographers an idea of what to strive for in shaping a dance. Secondly, the intent is to provide novices with the tools of the craft of choreography so that they will be able to vary and manipulate movements they have already discovered. Improvisation—the key to the choreographic process—is described in chapter 2. Improvisation is the ability to explore spontaneously and conceive dance movements that are representative of an idea, concept, or dance style. I desire that readers of this book can become comfortable with the improvisational process by following the various suggestions presented on this topic. Chapter 3 explains the craft of choreography in designing and shaping the dance.

Choreography: A Basic Approach Using Improvisation spans the process of dance composition form and provides explanations and examples of the process of creating a dance. A glossary of terms is provided at the end of the book. Each of these terms is italicized when first used in the text or when used in an important way. The final chapter, "The Finished Product: The Performance," describes ideas for blocking, costuming, and lighting a choreography for concert presentation. Additional suggestions are provided for organizing rehearsal schedules and putting together an informal performance.

Many of the dance concepts provided in this book can be used for modern, jazz, ballet, or tap dance choreography. Ideas are presented on a basic level that can be easily adapted to creative work in the different dance forms with their various terms and steps. Those who work with aerobics classes, drill teams, and cheerleading squads will also find the information in this text useful. More detailed comments have been provided throughout for the benefit of aerobics instructors.

Sandra Cerny Minton

Acknowledgments

Appreciation is extended to Bradford Beckwith, Suzanne Engle, Kevin Hadley, and Melinda Tatum who posed for the studio photographs found in this text.

Other University of Northern Colorado students appearing in this book include Kay Carara, Maryclaire Carara, Trish Coakley, Michael Coulson, Jeffrey Gallegos, Danielle Gautier, Gregory Gonzales, Sandra Greenhill, Lisa Groebe, James Hendricks, Judy Hoffman-Bejarano, Darlene LaPointe, Michael Larson, Eric Meyer, Elizabeth Robb, Paula Simpson, Steve Vattano, and Catherine Wettlaufer.

I also wish to thank Jackie S. Hill, lighting designer Dance '84 and '85 for her advice on the materials presented in the fifth section of chapter 4, and Lotus McElfish for her suggestions concerning the clarity of materials in this book.

The Guarded Soul *choreographed by Dale Lee Niven-Cooper. Photo courtesy of Bill Scherer.*

What Makes a Dance a Dance?

There is a special quality about a good piece of choreography that makes the observer want to get *involved*. In such a *dance*, the observer is lifted from his theater seat and transported along during the performance. But what distinguishes a good piece of *choreography* from a lesser work? What are some of the elements involved in creating and designing an effective dance—a dance that creates an illusion of being larger than life and that conveys a sense of magic and wonder?

Choreographic shape or form

One of the criteria of a good dance is that it has a *shape* or *form* to it—a form that progresses through time from the beginning to the end of the choreography. In learning how to choreograph, you need to develop a sense of how to give overall form to a composition. One way to describe the development of a dance is to say that the choreography has a beginning, middle, and conclusion or end (Hawkins, 1964). Each of these parts fits together to form a whole, with each part essential to that whole. In learning to compose a dance you are developing your ability to choose an appropriate beginning, middle, and end that relate to the form and feeling of the whole choreography.

Many smaller parts of movement comprise the *overall shape* of a dance *composition*. Generally these smaller pieces of movement are known as *phrases* and can be likened to the phrases that make up sentences in a written composition (Blom & Chaplin, 1982). The phrase, in fact, is the smallest unit of movement in the whole dance (Blom & Chaplin, 1982). As a beginning *choreographer*, it is necessary to develop a keen sense of phrasing.

A phrase of movement is marked by an *impulse* of *energy* that grows, builds, and finds a conclusion and that then *flows* easily and naturally into the next movement phrase in the dance. A phrase must have a natural sense of development about it. One action arbitrarily linked to the next will not form a well-constructed phrase of movements. Each of the separate movements comprising a phrase must be related (Blom & Chaplin, 1982). Many phrases make up a *section* in the choreography, and the sections together form the entire dance (Blom & Chaplin, 1982).

Movement phrases should contain *variety* in terms of their length and shape (Blom & Chaplin, 1982). When all phrases in a dance are of equal length—eight counts long, for example—phrasing becomes very predictable and boring for the audience. To have all phrases developed with the same shape also becomes monotonous.

One way you can practice phrasing movement is to allow your movement to be motivated by your breathing. As you breathe in, allow your breathing to move you in whatever *direction* you wish. Then let the next phrase of movement continue until you have finished exhaling. Practice breathing and moving with the breath, allowing your breathing to go into and propel different parts of your body. Make sure that all of your inhalations and exhalations are not of the same length.

Another method of developing a sense of phrasing is to allow yourself a certain number of *counts* for each phrase. For example, one phrase might be 10 counts long, whereas a second phrase is 16 counts long. Start with a movement in one part of your body and let it grow and build. Find a conclusion for this developing phrase at the end of the 10 counts, and immediately find another sequence that is 16 counts long. See if you can link the two phrases of unequal length so that as one concludes, the next one begins. It might help to have someone clap or beat a drum while you are devising your movement phrases. Someone could even count the number of beats to be included in each phrase. This would leave you free to concentrate on your movement and developing its direction.

Characteristics of a good dance

There is no single approach to providing a dance with a good sense of development, but certain common characteristics found in a well-formed piece of choreography can be identified and described.

It is essential that a dance have *unity* (Hawkins, 1964). This means that the separate movements in the choreography must fit or flow together and that each must be important to and contribute to the whole; phrases not essential to the *intent* of a work should be eliminated (Hawkins, 1964). An example of a dance lacking unity would be one in which the movements all seem to have the same *character* or ambience about them, but then suddenly a movement or series of movements appears that is very different in feeling. Such movements do not fit with the feeling of the choreography because they stand out as distinct from the *essence* of the piece and therefore interfere with the interconnectedness of the dance. It is easier for observers to absorb and get involved in a choreography that maintains unity because it has the capacity to attract and hold audience attention (Hawkins, 1964).

A second characteristic of a well-formed piece of choreography is *continuity*. A choreography with continuity has a sense of development that leads to a logical conclusion. It is in the process of happening, and the observer is swept along to its end (Hawkins, 1964).

Lyric Suite *choreographed by Sandra Minton. Photo courtesy of Bill Scherer.*

Such a dance provides a natural and organized progression of phrases so that one movement phrase flows naturally into the next; *transitions* from one sequence into another are not a problem (Hawkins, 1964). If progression from one phrase to another appears choppy or abrupt to the observer, transitions are probably poor. Poor transitions are distracting to the audience and interfere with its *involvement* in the performance of the dance (Hawkins, 1964). Poor transitions draw attention to the structure and design of the choreography rather than allowing the audience to focus on the overall feeling or form of the work as a whole.

To maintain audience interest, the choreographer must also provide *variety* within the development of a dance. The same phrase or movement performed again and again becomes tedious and boring. *Contrasts* in movement *forces* and spatial designs within the unity of a work add excitement (Hawkins, 1964). One way

Choreography: A Basic Approach Using Improvisation

to provide variety is to avoid repeating a movement phrase in exactly the same manner each time it is included in a work. In other words, the direction, sense of energy, or perhaps the *timing* of such a phrase could be changed so that it appears different to the audience when performed again in the same dance. Another technique for providing variety is to avoid repeating a movement or phrase on one side of the body when it has just been done on the other side of the body. Constant repetition of movement right-to-left or left-to-right is predictable and uninteresting to watch.

Some *repetition*, however, is important to dance form (Hawkins, 1964). Certain phrases do need to be repeated in a choreography so that the audience can see these movements again and identify with them. Repetition gives a feeling of *closure* to a work. It allows the audience to experience movements or phrases in greater depth because there is more familiarity with these repeated actions when they are seen again (Hawkins, 1964). Successful repetition of movements usually occurs later in the dance after other phrases have been presented in the intervening time period. You have probably guessed that a choreography must maintain a delicate balance of movements that use both variety and repetition. A dance consisting of totally different movement phrases following one another throughout the entire choreography would be just as ineffective as a choreography comprised of the continuous repetition of only several movement phrases. In the first situation, the audience cannot identify with the unending, unrelated string of movements, while in the latter instance movements in the dance become predictable. Too much variety destroys unity. Perhaps the key to balancing variety and repetition is to remember that variety is essential to good composition but must be provided with discrimination and in harmony with the overall nature of a work (Hawkins, 1964).

All the characteristics of a well-formed piece of choreography—unity, continuity, transition, variety, and repetition—are organized to contribute to the development of a meaningful whole. All phrases in a work should be designed to form the integrated sections of your dance, and all the parts of the dance should be placed in a *sequence* that moves toward an appropriate conclusion or closure. The development of a work should lead the audience logically from the beginning, to the middle, and on to the ending of the dance. The conclusion is the choreographer's own choice; it could be a surprise or an abrupt conclusion, or the dance could gradually fade from view.

Common choreographic forms

The overall shape of a piece of choreography can follow many different paths of development while still maintaining its sense of wholeness. Many possible dance forms have evolved through time based on musical forms developed at an earlier period.

A very simple choreographic form is one called the *AB*. This form consists of a beginning *section* called A, followed by a second section called B. While sections A and B fit together in terms of the common feeling of a composition, they each contain *elements* that are distinctly contrasting in *tone*. It could be said that sections A and B share some of the same ground but explore it from different points of view (Blom & Chaplin, 1982). A transition must be devised to link the two sections of a dance developed in the AB form. Such a transition could be presented abruptly, or it could be produced in a more gradual manner (Blom & Chaplin, 1982).

Another frequently used dance form is the *ABA*. This form has a sense of development that goes a step further than the AB. The ABA was derived from a musical form and has two sections, A and B, followed by

Jeux choreography by Elaine Vivace of the University of Nevada Las Vegas. Photo courtesy of Bill Scherer.

an ending A section. In the first part, *theme* A is stated and *manipulated*. Part B then presents a contrasting theme, and in the final section there is a return to theme A with a different twist (Horst & Russell, 1963). Louis Horst felt that a work that follows an ABA format is like life because it proceeds through the universal *pattern* of being born, living, and dying (Horst & Russell, 1963). All three sections A, B, and the return to A fit together to comprise a unified whole. There should be contrast between parts, yet they should be similar enough to suit the character of the entire dance. Section A, for example, could include large, broad movements, while part B, although choreographed in the same style, might use less *space* and energy. Part three, or the return to A, would be more expansive, but with somewhat different aspects than the original A. Skillful use of transition must again be provided between each of the three sections.

The *rondo* is a third common dance form. The rondo has many different sections following one after the other and can be described as an ABACADAEAFA development of movement *ideas* (Horst & Russell, 1963). The concept of a rondo is that there is an initial section A followed by an alternate or contrasting part B. The third section would be a return to A, either in its entirety or with some changes. The return to A would again be followed by a fourth section C, and another return to A. The remainder of the choreography includes parts D, E, and F interspersed with variations or restatements of A (Horst & Russell, 1963).

Theme and variations is a fourth dance form developed in a manner similar to the musical form with the same name. Here the choreographer must select a series of movements called the *theme*, which are then changed or varied throughout the development of the entire work (Humphrey, 1959).

The theme can be a single phrase of movements or several movement phrases put together in a sequence. In the theme and variations dance form, the theme or original movement series can be changed in a number of ways as the dance progresses, but the timing and sequence of the original theme remains (Blom & Chaplin, 1982). There should be no repetition of the original theme in its entirety (Blom & Chaplin, 1982). The theme and variations dance form is helpful to the choreographer because it provides a limited framework within which movement choices must be made (Humphrey, 1959).

A form of music called the *suite* is also used as a form in choreography. The most typical suite has a moderate beginning, a slow second part, and a fast, lively third section (Humphrey, 1959). Many pieces of music written in suite form are excellent accompaniment for dance.

The *narrative* form of choreography was very popular during the earlier years of *modern dance*. A narrative composition is sometimes known as a *story* or *dramatic dance*. Sometimes a narrative piece tells a simple story, but it can also communicate a tale of psychological relationships between dancers (Humphrey, 1959). Dramatic dances differ in length. Those for large groups of dancers and for more complicated ideas have been as long as an hour or more, while those choreographed for small groups or for a solo performer may be only minutes in length. The important aspect of the narrative choreographic form is that a consistent thread or purpose runs through the entire work (Humphrey, 1959).

The final dance form to be discussed is the *collage*. A collage consists of pieces of movement that are often unrelated but that have been brought together to create a whole (Blom & Chaplin, 1982). The effect created through this form is at times *surrealistic*, incongruous, *comic*, or even absurd; it especially lends itself to dances dealing with insanity or dreams (Blom & Chaplin, 1982). The movement ideas in a collage may seem disconnected, or body parts may appear to be disassociated from each other or from actions of the trunk as the dance is performed (Humphrey, 1959). In developing a collage, it is nevertheless necessary to have a point of *focus* in the actions with an overlapping or quick succession of movements (Blom & Chaplin, 1982).

There are additional methods of choreographing that can constitute a whole dance but that usually provide sufficient movement ideas for only a portion of a composition. These forms include the *canon, ground bass*, and dances devised by *chance*. A *canon* consists of one phrase of movement performed at different times by at least two different dancers, although many more performers could be used (Blom & Chaplin, 1982). In a canon, it is possible to have each dancer execute the entire phrase starting a number of counts behind another dancer (Blom & Chaplin, 1982). Each dancer could also begin the phrase at a different point in the series so that one dancer starts on count 2 while another starts on count 6 of that same phrase (Blom & Chaplin, 1982). In either case, a kind of overlapping visual and temporal effect is achieved.

The *ground bass* represents another choreographic technique. Ground bass is best described as a repetition of a movement phrase or phrases that are performed by a group. A soloist or smaller group then performs a more complex combination of movements at a position *downstage* of the larger group (Lockhart, 1982). A ground bass could also be performed in a circular form. Here the dancers outside the circle would be performing the repeated phrase, and the more complex and contrasting movements would be executed by a soloist or smaller group in the center of the circle. In either type of ground bass, the individuals performing the more complex movements could be exchanged with those in the larger group at various times throughout the piece.

Chance is another method of manipulating and developing movement. It was first employed by the well-known dancer Merce Cunningham. Dance by chance is a nontraditional choreographic method based on the idea that there is no prescribed order for a series of actions (Penrod & Plastino, 1980). In dances developed by chance, the choreographer gives up some of his direction and allows the dancers to make decisions about the content or organization of the work (Blom & Chaplin, 1982). Sometimes chance methods of determination, such as a throw of dice, are used to select movements for a dance or to give order to the phrases in a piece (Blom & Chaplin, 1982). Cunningham has also employed chance elements for the first time during an actual performance. One example of this is *Rainforest*, a dance in which Cunningham initially brought music and dance together during the *concert* (see Figure 1.1).

Selecting an appropriate form for a dance

The selection of a form for a dance is decided by the
choreographer. Dance form should be based on the nature and intent of a composition and should be suitable
to the feelings or ideas that you—the choreographer—
are trying to present. In the end, you may choose to
follow one of the dance forms already described, or
you may decide to develop your own unique form that
is more appropriate to your choreography. In either
case, it is important to perfect your skills so that you
have a good sense of development and understand
what constitutes a whole dance. Practice in construct-
ing dances based on a prescribed format, such as ABA
or theme and variations, is one way to refine your
sense of how to shape a dance. When you gain confi-
dence in working with these prescribed forms, you can
then dare to experiment with developmental ideas that
are more personal and more uniquely your own. Once
you have the ability to identify what works
choreographically, then you are free to mold a dance
as you see fit.

In order to choose an appropriate form for your
choreography, you need to identify what you are try-

Figure 1.2

Martha Graham and Bertram Ross in Appalachian Spring. *Uncredited photograph courtesy of the Dance Collection, The New York Public Library at Lincoln Center.*

Figure 1.3

Acrobats of God *performed by David Wood, Richard Kuch, and Helen McGehee. Photograph courtesy of the Dance Collection, The New York Public Library at Lincoln Center.*

ing to *project* to the audience. Making such decisions is extremely important to the *shaping* and forming process in dance composition because intent determines the shape that a choreography takes (Hawkins, 1964).

As has been described, in the early years of modern dance it was traditional to design a dance that told a story. Dances that contain a message or that communicate a story to the audience are known as *literal* choreography (Turner, 1971). A very famous modern dancer, Martha Graham, has done many full-length works that may be described as *dance dramas*. In these works the performers dance in the roles of specific characters and attempt to communicate a story or message to the audience. Examples of Graham's literal choreographies include pieces such as *Appalachian Spring* and *Acrobats of God*. The first of these dances portrays the drama of a young bride and her new husband taking possession of their home and beginning life together on the frontier. In the second choreography, Graham's intent was to communicate the problems and feelings encountered by a choreographer and the struggle involved in producing creative works (see Figures 1.2 and 1.3).

In more recent years the trend has been to move away from the literal in terms of choreographic form and *style*. Newer dances, particularly those from the 1970s, are based on *design* and *manipulation*; the main concern is experimenting with movement rather than relating a story. A dance deriving its intent from movement design is known as *nonliteral*. Nonliteral choreography communicates directly to the audience without explanations; its value is determined by its impact on the perceiver (Turner, 1971). Good examples of such pieces are the chance dances created by Cunningham. Cunningham himself has said that his intent is not to convey meanings to the audience but to experiment with movement and discover new dance forms (Blom & Chaplin, 1982).

There are dances, however, that cannot be perfectly classified as either literal or nonliteral. Such works do not tell a specific story, but they do draw inspiration from reality and thus could be considered *abstractions* from it (Hawkins, 1964). These dances draw from life and contain only the core or essence of the realistic *motivation* (Hawkins, 1964). An example of a dance that is an abstraction from life would be one about the sea or the seashore. In such a choreography, the dancers' movements would suggest the sea or hint at reactions to the seashore. There would be no movement included that depicted a *pantomime* of the waves or that portrayed activities traditionally done on a visit to the seashore. Instead, movements would suggest something more general that most people identify with when they think of the sea. A dance that is an abstraction from reality brings forth the essence of the original motivation; it contains a *semblance* of reality that we can identify but not put into words. Dances projecting an abstraction of reality were popular during the 1960s.

Whether a choreography is literal, nonliteral, or an abstraction from reality, a sense of form and intent is

Figure 1.4a

A typical jazz dance movement with bent knees and lowered center of weight. Photo courtesy of Jim Wanner.

Figure 1.4b

Jazz style kick. Photo courtesy of Jim Wanner.

still important. All movements should relate to the intent or motivation for creating a work regardless of whether that work is choreographed in a traditional or experimental framework. A sense of wholeness is also necessary. A choreography created with an integral synthesis of parts will be immediately recognized as such by the audience, even if some members of the audience are untrained in choreographic craft. Such a dance has the quality of being greater than life itself.

Dance style

A final motivation or intent for creating a dance is to follow a specific movement *style*. The form of such a choreography is determined by the style selected as its motivation. Overall shape could very well follow some of the forms described earlier in this chapter, or dance development could be of the choreographer's own design. Some common dance styles are *jazz, lyric, comic,* or *geometric*. Dance style, in particular, relates to the way *energy* and *rhythm* are arranged in a work, although the specific use of *line* and *shape* are integral aspects of dance style. In a well-done choreography it is easy to distinguish between various styles of movement.

Figure 1.5a

Lyric style movement. Note the softened or curved use of the arms. Photo courtesy of Jim Wanner.

Figure 1.5b

Another example of lyric movement. Photo courtesy of Jim Wanner.

Figure 1.5c

Same as 1.5b. Photo courtesy of Jim Wanner.

Jazz style dance has a *syncopated* rhythmic pattern similar to that of jazz music. Movement selected for a jazz dance is vital, energetic, and alive with a captivating energy and rhythm (Kraines & Kan, 1983). Jazz style dancing can be sharp or smooth but frequently involves movements known as *isolations* that are performed with only one part of the body (Kraines & Kan, 1983). It is difficult to resist the temptation to move yourself when watching jazz dance because the rhythms and energy are contagious (see Figures 1.4a and 1.4b).

In contrast to jazz dances, *lyric* dances are smooth, calm, and controlled. In fact, the movement style in lyric dance is very similar to that of classical ballet with a rounded use of line and shape. Lyric dancing is traditionally what many individuals imagine when they think about dance (see Figures 1.5a, 1.5b, and 1.5c).

Figure 1.6a

Typical movement from a comic choreography.
Photo courtesy of Jim Wanner.

Figure 1.6b

same as 1.6a. Photo courtesy of Jim Wanner.

Creating *comic* style dances requires a special out-look. Comedy does not need to involve the use of complex movement patterns and ideas but can grow from rather simple themes. To compose a comic dance, the choreographer must be able to see the unusual and funny in everyday happenings; comedy relies on an odd placement or juxtaposing of the elements of dance design (see Figures 1.6a and 1.6b).

Finally, a *geometric* style dance is one in which the emphasis is on line and shape. The style of dance described here is sometimes called *abstract*, but the word *geometric* is used in this book to avoid confusion with the word *abstraction*, which is a choreography based on the essence of something real. The process of abstraction from reality has been described above. Geometric dances are nonliteral; their goal is to

Figure 1.7a

Geometric style action emphasizing line, shape, and design. (Geometric dance is sometimes known as dance in an abstract style. The word geometric is used here to avoid confusion with dances that are based on an abstraction from reality.) Photo courtesy of Jim Wanner.

Figure 1.7b

same as 1.7a. Photo courtesy of Jim Wanner.

manipulate movement for its own sake, not to express feeling or intent. When watching a geometric style work, the observer is drawn into an involvement with visual designs and with impulses and control of energy. The main concern in geometric style dance is how the choreographer manipulates these factors in the dance space. Figures 1.7a and 1.7b show examples of the geometric style.

As choreographer you may decide to compose a literal dance that tells a story or one that is strictly nonliteral. You may even mix some of the dance forms and styles described so that your jazz or lyric style composition also communicates a story to the audience. Whatever your motivation in creating a choreography, it is important for the dance form you choose to fit your intent.

Choosing appropriate subject matter

Because the form or development of a choreography grows from its motivating idea, the choice of appropriate subject matter is very important for the development of a successful composition. Dance is very ephemeral (Humphrey, 1959). The nature of its media—movement—causes it to be so. Movement is seen, and then it is gone. It must be remembered through the *images* of the mind so that each mental picture adds up in the viewer's memory to form a whole dance that is a complete work of art.

Complex subjects are usually inappropriate for choreography. Simple, action-oriented ideas provide much better motivation for dance composition because they can be presented and developed more easily (Humphrey, 1959). Such motivating and action-oriented ideas are also understood and remembered more readily by the audience. Philosophical ideas, for example, can be described more effectively through words or a combination of words and actions (Humphrey, 1959). The famous choreographer Doris Humphrey has made the following additional observations concerning the selection of choreographic motivation. Humphrey maintains that in dance (a) the idea of propaganda or social reform is overwhelming; (b) cosmic themes such as the creation of the world are too vast; (c) mechanical ideas lead to very mechanical, technique-oriented compositions; and (d) literary stories are too complex in terms of the interpersonal relationships involved to be easily translated into movement, particularly by the beginning choreographer (Humphrey, 1959).

A dance title

A dance title is a guidepost for the audience. It sets the stage and points the way, indicating in general what is to come and what the audience can expect from a choreography. A title, however, should leave some of the mystery about a dance intact, allowing members of the audience to explore their curiosity and imagination concerning the work (Ellfeldt, 1967). In choosing a title for a dance, leave enough latitude for members of the audience to experience the choreography on their own terms. Good names for dances are often suggested by the title or style of the accompaniment, the style of the choreography, or a relationship created between the performers. A dance title and program notes should grow from the motivating materials with which the choreographer has been working; they should not merely describe the action of the dance (Ellfeldt, 1967).

Learning to choreograph takes time

Developing your choreographic abilities takes time and occurs in developmental stages (Hawkins, 1964). It is a trial-and-error process of seeing, experiencing, and learning. Viewing good choreography in performance is one way to heighten your sensitivity and gain a better understanding of how to mold and give form to your work. You will probably be asked to put together many short dances in your choreography class. Each of these short pieces is known as a *study* and usually deals with some specific aspect of the composition process. In each study you will be working on the forming and shaping process in order to gain a better sense of what makes up a whole dance. Some specific suggestions about creating different kinds of studies will be provided in the following chapters. The first step in creating either a study or a whole dance is to discover appropriate movement through the process of *improvisation*. The improvisation process will be described in chapter 2. Your teacher can also provide you with many helpful suggestions concerning choreographic development.

A word about aerobic dance

Much of what has been said in this chapter applies to art dance composition rather than to choreography for aerobics. Nevertheless, some of the suggestions can be helpful for those who put together aerobics routines.

An aerobics routine does not have the same development or overall form as an art dance choreography. The goal in aerobics is to build cardiovascular endurance through vigorous exercise. In art dance, the goal is to create a dance that cohesively develops from a beginning, through a middle, and on to the end of the composition. All phrases in an art dance contribute to and are integral to the whole. In aerobics such an organic sense of development is not really necessary, although it is more interesting to place movement sequences that make beginning and ending statements at appropriate points in the routine.

All movement sequences or phrases in an aerobics dance generally consist of repeating the same step or movement a certain number of times. This is followed by another vigorous step that is again performed repeatedly. Interest could be added to aerobics routines by including phrases of differing lengths. One could also add interest by giving some of the phrases a simple sense of development instead of merely repeating the same step or movement.

The comments on dance style in this chapter could also be applied to aerobic dance. It is fun to experiment with routines in jazz, comic, or country swing styles. Many of the steps shown in books on aerobics can be easily adapted to music of different styles while still supplying the required amount of vigorous activity. In addition, movement in a lyric style, together with appropriate music, could be used for the warm-down activity at the conclusion of an aerobics class.

Civilized Evil *choreographed by Catherine Wettlaufer. Photo courtesy of Bill Scherer.*

The Process: Finding The Right Movement

Discovering movement is the first step in beginning to choreograph a dance. Later these movements can be manipulated and shaped into a well-designed composition using your knowledge of the choreographic *craft*.

Discovery of appropriate movement is accomplished through *improvisation*. In improvisation, the choreographer moves spontaneously while concentrating on the intent of a choreography. The choreographer is guided in improvisation by the initial motivation selected for composing a dance (Hawkins, 1964).

Concentration and relaxation

As a beginning choreographer, there are many things you can do to perfect your improvisational skills. The first of these is to strengthen the connection between your mind and body by developing your ability to concentrate. Through better concentration, you will be able to identify and recall movements that come to you during the improvisational process.

Concentration is enhanced by the ability to relax. The ability to relax appears to make an individual more receptive to movement ideas and *images* as they come forth. Psychologist Richard Suinn of Colorado State University has put forth considerable effort to improve the performance of athletes. In his work, Suinn has used the imagery of a mental rehearsal of a successful performance to help bring out the best execution of movement skills in each competitor. Concentration on mental imagery, however, is preceded by exercises in deep relaxation (Bry, 1978). Suinn believes that the key to tuning in to your mental imagery stems from this ability to relax (Bry, 1978).

Authors who have written about creative work also discuss a certain state of mind that they have found to be compatible with successful creative work or problem solving. This state of mind is partway between the conscious and the unconscious mind; it is a state in which daydreaming and reveries take place (Rugg, 1963). In his book *Imagination*, Harold Rugg indicated that creating requires one to find the threshold level of a mental state in which the mind is off-guard, relaxed, and receiving messages or ideas related to the creative work at hand (Rugg, 1963).

Many popular courses in stress reduction employ relaxation techniques. The Jacobson Progressive Relaxation system suggests that the individual alternately tense and relax specific parts of the body in order to distinguish sensations of tension from relaxed feelings (Jacobson, 1929). Progressive Relaxation enables the individual to identify points of tension in the body that can be worked on to release tension. Persons who have little or no sensitivity to body tension gradually allow these tensions to accumulate. Over time such persons accommodate to these tensions unaware of their building intensity.

Another good relaxation technique is to concentrate on your breathing. This is best accomplished while lying on the floor in a position as relaxed as possible. Next begin to concentrate on inhaling and exhaling and practice this several times. Try deepening your breathing to the pelvic floor. Next experiment with breathing into different parts of your body, particularly into those body parts that retain tension (Dowd, 1981). Then return to your normal breathing rhythm.

Mental images that suggest relaxing scenes are also helpful for releasing tension. Such images might include lying on a featherbed or on a beach on a warm summer day. Relaxing images could also be the idea of floating or hovering above the ground. Martin Rossman, a medical doctor, and David Bresler, a psychologist, have done considerable work with mental imagery. They call their technique "guided imagery." In this relaxation system, clients are coached in various exercises that improve their ability to focus on their mental imagery for the purpose of taking better care of themselves (Rossman and Bresler, 1983). Some of these exercises also involve relaxation. In one exercise individuals are encouraged to take several slow and very deep breaths, breathing from the abdomen. With each exhalation the patient is told to imagine himself taking in energy from the universe and then to sense his body as becoming more relaxed. Finally the patient is encouraged to imagine the inside of his body to be growing brighter and more radiant from the center outward (Samuels & Bennett, 1973). This exercise should induce a feeling of relaxation and increased energy and can be practiced during a short pause in an individual's otherwise busy day.

Finally, concentration and the mind-body connection are improved by learning to pay attention in dance technique class. Do not allow your mind to wander while practicing dance technique. When you find this happening, pull your mind back and attempt to identify the body feelings, sensations, and tensions you are experiencing while doing particular movements. At the same time, try to remain as relaxed as possible while still maintaining your concentration.

Beginning with exploration

One way to develop competence in dance improvisation is to experience movement *exploration* first. Like improvisation, movement exploration is a spontaneous process, and the movements that come forth are

Lyric Suite *choreographed by Sandra Minton. Photo courtesy of Bill Scherer.*

unplanned. Movement exploration is also guided by intent or suggestion as the basis for the movements that are done. The difference between exploration and improvisation is that improvisation is a much more in-depth process (Hawkins, 1964). Exploration is usually guided by the teacher, whereas improvised movement is motivated by the ideas, memories, and images of the dancer. In exploration, the dancer can concentrate on the way in which his or her body moves. Improvisation is a deeper process in which movement is drawn from more personal and internally oriented cues (Hawkins, 1964). Some examples of movement exploration experiences follow. You may want to try some of these exercises with your eyes closed to heighten your ability to concentrate. Your teacher will also provide you with opportunities to explore.

Sit quietly on the floor with your legs crossed. Concentrate on your right arm and allow it to begin to move. Try moving your arm in different directions and at different levels in relation to your body. Explore possible movements in the parts of your arm such as the

Choreography: A Basic Approach Using Improvisation

shoulder, elbow, or wrist. See how many different ways each joint area moves. Lift your arm to the side of your body and trace a shape such as a circle in space. Try tracing other shapes such as triangles or zigzag lines at the side of your body. Concentrate on connecting the flow of energy from your torso with energy in your arm. Allow this energy to flow back and forth between the center and periphery of your body (Hawkins, 1964).

Your sensation of gravity can also motivate an interesting series of movement explorations. Again begin from a position in which you are sitting on the floor and are relatively relaxed. Allow your body to begin lifting *very slowly* off the floor and concentrate on the feeling of gravity as it pulls down on the parts of your body. Feel gravity's pull and heaviness as you arise. Sense your body growing taller as you lift off the floor. When you are reaching as tall as you can, descend slowly back to the floor (Hawkins, 1964). Again be aware of your body tensions throughout this entire process. As a variation in this exercise, try lifting only one part of your body away from the floor, again focusing on gravity as it pulls down that body part.

A movement exploration experience can be developed from practice in aligning the body. Lie down on the floor and decide how it feels to you to have all parts of your body aligned. Take this sense of alignment to a sitting and then to a standing position. Feel the placement of the head, shoulders, torso, and hips as they are positioned right above your base of support, the feet. Allow yourself to slump forward from the waist, and then slowly uncurl the body to a tall standing position (Hawkins, 1964). Try this slumping and uncurling action at a fast and then at a medium rate of speed as well. Perform the action intermittently rather than continuously. Finally, explore other torso movements, such as stretching diagonally or twisting in the waist. Concentrate on how each of these actions feels to you.

Following and *mirroring* also provide enjoyable exploration experiences while developing a dancer's ability to perceive movement at the same time. Stand behind another dancer and attempt to follow and replicate the dancer's actions. Be aware of the shape and development of the dancer's movements. Connect one shape to the next, being sensitive to energy flow and impulses.

Mirroring is done while you are facing another person. In a mirroring experience, one person is designated as the leader. The other person attempts to mirror the leader's movements. It is also necessary for the leader to remain facing the partner while moving. In both mirroring and following exercises, movement must remain relatively slow in order to enhance concentration between parties; the person following should not attempt to think ahead to anticipate the leader's movements. It is much better simply to experience shapes and energies within actions as they occur.

Another exploration technique is one in which students experiment with different uses of space, time, or energy. This exercise is begun by moving on a basic *pulse* or beat. The pulse could be supplied by the basic beat of a piece of recorded music or by the beating of a percussion instrument. Try changing the *level* or direction of your movements every eight counts, every four counts, and then every two counts. Next, try making changes in the *tempo* of your movements at similar intervals, or hold a position for a certain number of counts before continuing on with your movement on the pulse. Additional suggestions for explorations are listed below.

1. Stand in a comfortable position and concentrate on your right arm. Allow an impulse of energy to move your arm. Try applying differing amounts of energy to your arm, and notice where your arm travels (Hawkins, 1964). Be sensitive to the tensions and muscular feelings associated with different shadings and uses of energy. Do this exploration in other parts of your body.

2. Rest quietly in what you consider to be a well-aligned stance. Be aware that your body sways slightly in order to maintain a normal standing position. Throw your hips to one side so that they extend beyond your base of support. Experiment with shifting your hips in forward, backward, side, and diagonal directions (Hawkins, 1964). Determine how far you have to shift your hips in a particular direction before you lose your balance and fall. Note that balance can be maintained by shifting your hips in one direction and your upper body in another (Hawkins, 1964). Play with the sensation of being on and then off balance by shifting a part of your body out of alignment. Allow yourself to go off center and take as many steps as needed to regain your balance. Try this several times so that losing and recovering your balance cause you to trace a pathway in space.

3. Move slowly around the dance space and be aware of how your total *alignment* tilts forward. Maintaining good posture is more difficult while you are moving (Hawkins, 1964). Practice changing the degree of tilt of your whole body as you move. Shift only a single part of your body out of line while you are moving and see what happens. Change the speed of your locomotion from slow

to fast and back to slow again to see how this affects your ability to travel across space.

4. Pick a simple movement that can be executed with one arm. This movement could be a *swinging* action or the tracing of a shape in space. Experiment with making this same movement as large as possible. Next see how small this movement can be made. Finally choose a *size* for this movement that is between what you consider to be large and small. See if you can change movement size without stopping. Then try this same exploration with another part of your body.

Improvising

Improvisation is a more complete and inner-motivated experience than exploration (Hawkins, 1964). In improvisation, the creator has a hand in selecting the motivation or at least parts of the motivation for movement and often relies on the use of memories and past experiences as a stimulus for action. There are more opportunities to vary the movements during improvisation. Improvisation also involves the process of feeling and forming. The dancer is expected to be aware of the overall shape of his or her movements in order to gain understanding of what makes up a beginning, middle, and appropriate closure or ending for dance actions. A successful improvisation should leave the individual with a feeling of unity and self-realization (Hawkins, 1964).

Improvisations can be initiated by a number of different sources or *stimuli*. These stimuli can be visual, auditory, tactile, or *kinesthetic*. In addition, various kinds of imagery and *props* can also be used to facilitate improvisational experiences. Examples of each type of movement stimuli follow:

1. Visual
   - Pictures from magazines and books.
   - Colored paper cut into different shapes.
   - Various kinds of line patterns such as scallops, zigzags, spirals, or a combination of these.
   - Interesting natural objects, including shells, pine cones, leaves, or starfish (Hawkins, 1964).

2. Auditory
   - Recorded music, particularly modern or *electronic* sound.
   - Percussive music played live in the dance studio on drums, cymbals, bells, tambourines, or any other instrument you may want to experiment with.
   - Body sounds such as slapping, clapping, or snapping the fingers.
   - Foot sounds or rhythmic patterns.
   - Vocal sounds such as hissing, clacking the tongue, or whistling.
   - Nonsense syllables, words, or even poetry or prose phrases.
   - Words with kinesthetic qualities such as ooze, melt, soar, collapse, or dart (Ellfeldt, 1967).

3. Tactile
   - Objects having interesting qualities to the touch such as furry, slimy, slippery, sharp, or soft.
   - Nature objects with interesting tactile qualities.
   - Objects providing for tactile and spatial explorations such as a chair, the inside of a large box, or the corner of the dance studio.

Figure 2.1

A skirt extends and heightens movements of the legs. Photo courtesy of Jim Wanner.

4. Kinesthetic

   • Pedestrian movements from daily life, including walking, running, lifting, or falling.

   • Waving, saluting, shaking hands, and other gestures from life experiences (Humphrey, 1959).

   • Movements such as leaping, skipping, or turning learned in a dance *technique* class.

   • *Combinations* of movement from dance technique classes.

   • Various spatial paths traced on the floor.

   • The spelling of words or names in space or as a floor pattern.

5. Imagery

   Imagery can be quite varied, but in each case it should constitute an imaginary motivation rather than something existing in the real world. Memories and past experiences often play a strong part in defining a person's imagery and in enabling one to move in relation to it. If it is to be successful, imagery used for improvisation should be meaningful for those involved.

Figure 2.2

Hoops can frame and emphasize movements and shapes made with the body. Photo courtesy of Jim Wanner.

- Imagery of beautiful scenery, such as a day spent in the mountains.

- Kinesthetic or body feelings, including the feeling of lying on a warm comfortable mattress or having your feet on a hot sidewalk.

- Improvisations from dramatic situations such as pretending that you are being chased by someone or that you are finding your way across a darkened room.

- Imagining yourself within unusual environments such as the inside of a block of Swiss cheese or the inside of a piano (Hanstein, 1980). (When using dramatic imagery or the idea of unusual environments, the teacher should verbally paint the mental picture of each situation very clearly.)

6. Props
   - Various pieces of clothing pulled from the costume closet or brought from home, including capes and skirts of different lengths and fullness (see Figure 2.1).

   - Pieces of material draped on the body in a variety of ways.

   - Hoops of varying colors (see Figure 2.2).

Figure 2.3

Scooters used in children's physical education classes provide playful and creative props for choreography. Photo courtesy of Jim Wanner.

Figure 2.4

The choreographer can use sticks to extend visual design or to add sound effects to a dance. Photo courtesy of Jim Wanner.

- Scooters used in children's physical education classes (see Figure 2.3).

- Sticks and poles of varying lengths and thicknesses (see Figure 2.4).

- Elastic bands stretched in many directions (see Figure 2.5). (The elastic bands need to be about

Figure 2.5

Use of elasticized bands to create designs in space. Nikolais Dance Theatre performing Tensile Involvement. *Uncredited photo courtesy of the Dance Collection, The New York Public Library at Lincoln Center.*

Figure 2.6

An example of a sack-like costume that can be pulled and stretched in many directions. Nikolais Dance Theatre in Group Dance *from* Sanctum. *Uncredited photo courtesy of the Dance Collection, The New York Public Library at Lincoln Center.*

2 to 2-1/2 inches wide and large enough in size to surround a dancer's body.)

- Elasticized sacks covering the body (see Figure 2.6). (Such sacks can be pulled into a variety of shapes.)
- Scarves and streamers of different lengths to create designs in space as a dancer moves.

Figure 2.7
A chair is another useful prop for the choreographer.
Photo courtesy of Jim Wanner.

One important factor to remember in selecting a motivation for dance improvisation is that it should lend itself to or suggest movement fairly easily. Nouns such as "rock" or suggestions such as "sit" or "stand" do not hold much potential for inspiring movement improvisations. How can one move while trying to create the impression of being a rock? Waves or a river, on the other hand, have far greater potential as imagery to stimulate movement.

A second factor to remember in selecting a worthwhile motivation for improvisation is that it should be appropriate for a specific group. Stimuli used with 8-year-old children would probably not appeal to college students. The background and experiences of class members must be considered, and improvisational experiences must be structured for those at a particular learning level (Hawkins, 1964).

The following descriptions are provided as examples of improvisational experiences. Notice in each example how much more freedom is allowed than in exploration for the creator to supply his or her own ideas. Compare these improvisational experiences with the work in movement exploration previously described.

Auditory stimuli are fun to experiment with and provide accompaniment for the movement at the same time. Move around the room trying out the different body sounds you can make, such as slapping, clapping, and snapping the fingers. Pick two or three of the body sounds that you like best. Play with these sounds, combining them with appropriate movements. Allow your movements to vary in direction, size, level, and tempo. Change and vary the order of these sounds and movements, finally selecting an order that you like. Continue experimenting with the sequence you have chosen, developing a *rhythmic pattern* as you move by performing some of your actions more slowly and other actions faster than the underlying pulse (Hawkins, 1964). Allow time for *silences* in which you hold a shape or body position; attempt to return to movement on the pulse beat from time to time (Hawkins, 1964). Practice the sounds and rhythmic pattern as you move around the dance space, and notice the rhythmic patterns being performed by the other dancers. See if you can pick up their rhythmic patterns; then return to your own pattern. As you move, continue to pick up other rhythmic patterns when you feel like it. At times extend one of these patterns and develop it into a longer sequence.

The use of a prop can provide you with many interesting movements. Begin your improvisation by learning how your prop moves. Experiment with varying uses of space, time, and energy. Allow your body to travel in different directions and at different levels as you continue to move your prop. Take note of the ways in which the prop changes or extends the movement of your body. Discover other ways to move with the prop. When you have developed many of the possibilities, start to bring your movement to an ending (Hawkins, 1964). Let this closing happen naturally (see Figures 2.1-2.7).

Another example of an improvisation is one stemming from your reactions to a beautiful natural object—a seashell. Begin by picking up the shell and examining it carefully. Try to sense all of its qualities, including its color, *texture*, shape, line, and design.

Experience both the visual and the tactile qualities of this shell, exploring its qualities inside and out.

Put the shell down and move off to your own space in the dance studio. Concentrate on your sensations of and feelings about the seashell. Be quiet initially. Develop an ability to be sensitive to yourself and to your images. Move only when you feel ready and motivated to do so. You might want to have your eyes closed at first and then open them as you increase your ability to concentrate on your impulses for action. After you have improvised for a while, find an appropriate conclusion for your movement.

Movement exploration is a more outer-motivated experience than improvisation. It develops from the teacher's or *facilitator's* suggestions rather than from those motivations that are based on feelings or reactions to stimuli for movement. In exploration, movement grows from a more concrete basis and is easier to handle when one is first learning how to move spontaneously. It is easier to learn how to improvise by doing explorations first. Movement exploration should be followed by improvisations of a more physical or concrete nature such as those that call for relating to auditory stimuli or experimenting with a prop like the hoop. The improvisation dealing with feeling reactions to a shell is an example of a more inner-motivated experience and should be introduced later. Early improvisational experiences need to be more structured, whereas later experiences can allow dancers more freedom to respond individually to the motivation (Hawkins, 1964). It might also be worthwhile to repeat feeling-oriented improvisations because it may take more practice before individuals can get involved in and relate spontaneously to these ideas (Hawkins, 1964).

Additional suggestions on improvisation

Finding and maintaining the right mental state is important for successful improvisation to occur. As already indicated, the right mental state during improvisation is one in which the dancer is concentrating yet relaxed. There needs to be sufficient concentration so that mind and body are synchronized and the mind is open to the impulses and flow of movement ideas from the body (Rugg, 1963). Excessive concentration and effort create too much tension, however, blocking the pathway between mind and body.

You can do several things to create conditions that facilitate the kind of mind-body connection desirable in an involved improvisation session. One thing is to find an environment—a room or place—in which you can move comfortably. This should be a room in which you feel content and "tuned into" yourself. You should consider size, shape, color, temperature, floor surface, and other factors in selecting an appropriate space for your creative work. Experiment with different spaces for your improvisations before you select one.

A teacher can also do a great deal to create an atmosphere conducive to creative work. Improvisation works best in an environment of "openness" where the dancers feel free to try and to dare (Hawkins, 1964). Dancers doing an improvisation should be able to experiment with movement without the worry of being evaluated. In improvisation sessions, evaluation should be internal rather than external (Hawkins, 1964).

Another important factor in creating the right atmosphere for improvising is the time of day you choose to work. If you think about your progression through each day, you will find that there are certain times of day when you feel "up" and are most productive. These are the times of day when you are most alert and are probably the times when you should do your improvising. It is hard to work creatively when you feel dull, bored, or sleepy.

Once you begin improvising, allow your body to go with the flow of energy that comes forth. Try not to think too hard or to anticipate actions as they develop from your motivation; just let movement happen (Hawkins, 1964). Dance is a nonverbal experience, and excessive thinking blocks the body's energy flow. This ability to go with the flow of creative work may be described as "turning off the conscious mind" and coming to a mental state that is more global and less detail oriented. It is a state in which the individual is poised between the conscious and subconscious— receptive to images and messages from within, but in control from without (Rugg, 1963). Continued practice in improvisation will help you to identify and summon this receptive state. It takes many sessions before you are able to connect readily with the condition of mind and body that allows movement to flow forth freely. Learn to be still, concentrating on inner impulses for movement. You need to go with the flow and avoid forcing the process.

Closing the eyes often helps to increase concentration. When you first begin doing improvisations, try moving while your eyes are closed (Hawkins, 1964). For many people, moving with the eyes closed cuts out external distractions and heightens receptivity to internal and personal images. Once you have connected with the appropriate feelings of concentration, open your eyes and continue to move while attempting to maintain your inward focus.

Proper mental imagery or visualization is very important in many but not all improvisations. As you are improvising, sensitize yourself to mental pictures as they appear in your mind. These pictures usually evolve from the motivation with which you are working. Learn to focus on the images in your mind so that you can recall a picture that was particularly interesting or important to you. Practice moving while you concentrate on your mental images to see what kind of movements come forth.

The dance study

A *study* is a short dance. As such it should have all the attributes of good choreography described in chapter 1. You will have many opportunities to do studies in your dance composition classes. The first step in creating a dance study is to discover appropriate movement through improvisation. Again it is important to know your intent or motivation so that you can concentrate on it when finding movement.

Many students have trouble remembering movements that come to them during an improvisation session. This problem can be solved through practice. Remembering improvised movement is important because later these movements will need to be molded and formed into a study or piece of choreography. Movement memory is heightened through repetition. When you find a movement phrase or phrases that feel right to you, go back and try to do the movements again. Keep repeating these movements until their shape and phrasing seem to fit your imagery and motivation. You will find that the ability to remember movement is comparable to standing outside yourself and watching yourself improvise. As you repeat movements that seem right to you, you will find that they begin to be clarified. Your movements will gradually take shape so that the spatial pathways, step patterns, and use of arms, head, body, and focus develop to your liking and feel "right" to you. The ability to give form to a study or dance takes time. Each individual needs the proper environment and enough practice and encouragement; no two people can be expected to pass through the levels of choreographic development in the same way or at the same rate of speed (Hawkins, 1964).

Most of the motivations described earlier as a basis for improvisations could be molded into a dance study or a fully formed dance. You might also experiment with some of the ideas suggested for exploring movement to see if you can develop a dance or study using these ideas as motivation.

Dealing with blocks to creativity

On some days you will find that your work in improvisation flows easily. Movement ideas come forth and fit with the intent of your choreography. At other times, improvising will be much more difficult, and you will feel "blocked." At such times you will need to be patient with yourself. You cannot expect your mind and body to be equally receptive at all times. Because a dance takes shape in stages, allow yourself enough time for your creative urges to incubate and emerge. Realize that it may be better to put your work on a composition aside and come back to it at a later date.

You will also discover that movement ideas do not always come forth in a logical manner. For example, the ending of a dance may come to you before the middle is completed. Again, have patience. Be aware of the evolving shape of your dance and its development from beginning to end. Gradually, you will know where various movement materials fit. As you discover phrases through improvisation, you will also find where to place them in the progression of your piece.

Finally, be careful not to force a composition into a specific format or overall shape. Let choreographic form develop naturally in relation to your motivating ideas. If a piece seems to be taking shape in a certain direction, explore that direction even though it may differ from your original intent. The important goal is for the dance to fit together with a sense of wholeness and grow from a natural or *organic* development of movements and phrasing.

Accompaniment

Many different kinds of music are appropriate as accompaniment for dance. The key in selecting dance music, however, is to find accompaniment that fits the motivation or intent of your choreography. Although a dance should not mimic or parrot musical structure, it is important that the two—music and dance—have a similarity in terms of basic feeling (Humphrey, 1959).

Other criteria should be considered when selecting music as accompaniment for dance. Instrumental music usually provides better accompaniment because it provides greater freedom for choreographic interpretation. The tendency when using vocal music, particularly with beginning choreographers, is to pantomime the words rather than to draw movement from inner feelings as motivation (Blom & Chaplin, 1982).

Additional suggestions concerning musical selection are to find accompaniment with variety in structure, rhythmic patterning, and quality. The tendency is to select repetitious movement when working with music that has little variety. Secondly, large instrumental groups such as a symphony orchestra are usually not appropriate for dance accompaniment. An entire orchestra overpowers the movement of a small number of dancers; such accompaniment requires a large number of performers in a piece in order to complement the volume and intensity of the music (Humphrey, 1959). Small musical groups such as a trio or quartet usually provide excellent accompaniment for dance.

Finally, it is advisable to avoid popular music for your dance compositions. Much of this music does not leave freedom for choreographic interpretation because it has been played continuously on the radio. People in your audience will have heard these pieces many times and may have preconceived ideas of how one should dance to them (Humphrey, 1959).

The recommendations concerning musical selection in the previous paragraphs refer primarily to accompaniment for art dance. Music for aerobics routines should have a high energy level that can motivate participants to continue vigorous activity for a period of time. Popular music is frequently appropriate and is often preferred for aerobic dance. As long as the accompaniment is lively, vocal selections do not interfere with the enthusiasm of those in a class. Variety in musical style is suggested to build group enthusiasm.

It is important to investigate a variety of sources to find appropriate accompaniment. Local music stores or libraries can be good sources of ideas, particularly if they carry a selection of classical, semiclassical, jazz, and modern or electronic recordings. The music of a flute, harp, or percussion ensemble can be inspiring; your FM radio can be another source of musical ideas. Listen carefully to FM stations and learn to keep notes on the title, composer, and record label of selections that appeal to you. Later you can order them at a record shop or find them in a music library. Music collections owned by friends can also offer some ideas. You might investigate ethnic music from different countries and musical selections from different historical periods such as the medieval era as additional sources for dance accompaniment. It is also possible to compose your own music or have someone compose it for you. Such accompaniment could be traditional or modern in sound, or it could be developed from words and nonsense syllables that were recorded or recited by the dancers as they performed the piece.

It is important to know the structure of your music when you begin to improvise. Listen to your accompaniment carefully; be familiar with its musical phrasing, rhythmic patterning, and tone or feeling. If you are using metrically organized music, know how many counts are in each measure. Most pieces of music are written in 2/4, 3/4, 4/4, or 6/8 *meter* or in *mixed meter* so that the measures vary in the number of counts included in each bar or grouping (see Figure 2.8). Electronic music is not usually organized with a tight metric structure and can provide the choreographer with a much greater range of dance interpretations than musical accompaniment of a more structured nature (Turner, 1971). You still need to be aware, however, of how such music is developed and what feelings it evokes.

In choreographing aerobics routines, it is also important to consider the music's style and meter. You will need to try out different steps with the selected accompaniment to see how they fit with the music. Some movements may not work at all. Transitions between different step patterns must be considered, too, so that vigorous action can continue without interruption.

Begin choreographing your dance by listening to your music. Relax and concentrate on basic ideas or feelings the music brings to mind. Continue to concentrate, allowing yourself to begin improvising. You will find that certain movements and movement pat-

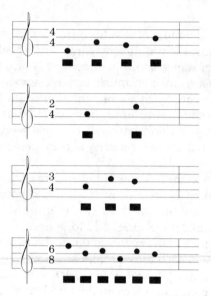

Figure 2.8

It is important for a choreographer to understand how a piece of music is organized. The dashes indicate the number of underlying beats in each measure for different time signatures.

terns come forth. Remember these movements, and if necessary write them down. Later these movements can be varied and manipulated to form an entire composition.

While you improvise, turn the music off for a while. Continue to improvise in order to clarify your movements. Then return to your accompaniment, performing the movement with the music (Blom & Chaplin, 1982). You may find yourself repeating this process of concentrating and improvising many times throughout the development of your choreography.

Ideally, the relationship between a dance and its accompaniment should be complementary; one should not dominate the other, and each should have a form of its own. The dance and music should have similar styles and evoke similar feelings in the observer, but the dance should not mirror musical structure in movement. The dance and accompaniment should relate and synthesize at certain points throughout the development of a choreography so that the two coexist in a mutually supportive relationship (Blom & Chaplin, 1982).

All in Time *choreographed by Karen Genoff Campbell. Photo courtesy of Bill Scherer.*

The Craft: Designing and Shaping the Dance

Once you have found movement and movement phrases through improvisation, then you can begin to *design* your dance. This is the point at which the craft of choreography becomes important.

Choreographic *craft* implies the ability of the choreographer to give form to his or her piece so that the dance has a sense of wholeness. A knowledge of craft also involves the process of movement *manipulation*—the varying and extending of movement. The ability to vary movement phrases means that the choreographer can use a movement phrase more than once in a work without becoming repetitious. Because the movement phrase is changed in appearance when presented a second or even a third time in a dance, it will still be interesting for the audience to watch.

Finally, craft in dance composition means that the choreographer knows where to place the dancers in the stage space to achieve maximum effect. Appropriate placement of dancers on the stage heightens the projection of movement and creates meaningful visual and kinesthetic relationships between the performers. Movement can be easily hidden from the audience when a dancer is placed in a weak stage area or told to *face* in the wrong direction.

Movement manipulation and variation

Manipulation means varying movements through an understanding of space, time, energy, and shape in dance composition. Each of these *elements* is an important aspect of all human actions. Movement occurs in

Figure 3.1
Facing in different directions creates a varied effect for the audience. The dancer facing the back lacks the feeling and expression projected by the other three dancers. Photo courtesy of Jim Wanner.

space, takes time, is propelled by energy, and goes through a series of specific shapes as it is executed by performers.

Space. The movement element *space* can be divided into smaller categories because it includes the aspects of direction, size, level, and focus. There are many different *directions* in which movement can go in dance, such as forward, to either side, and backwards. Human movement can also travel in a variety of diagonal directions, including the two diagonals that extend in front of the body and the two diagonals extending in back of the body. A dancer can move the body in all eight of these directions, or he can simply *face* the body in any of the eight directions (see Figure 3.1).

Human movement has great possibilities in terms of variation in *size*. Almost any action can be larger or smaller than originally executed. *Level* can be changed too, and in dance the level of a movement is generally designated as either high, medium, or low. A change of the dancer's *focus* can also change the appearance of a phrase because an individual can focus in many different directions while still performing the same movement series (see Figures 3.2a, 3.2b, and 3.2c).

Figure 3.2a

The three dancers demonstrate a gradually widening or larger movement from right to left. Photo courtesy of Jim Wanner.

Figure 3.2b

There are three basic levels of movement— high, middle, and low. Photo courtesy of Jim Wanner.

Figure 3.2c

Changing focus from low to high alters the appearance of a similar body shape or movement. Photo courtesy of Jim Wanner.

You can learn to vary movement in the following manner. Select a simple floor pattern that carries you on a pathway across and around the dance space. This floor pattern could be a spiral, zigzag, or combination of the two. Practice your floor pattern first using walking steps to trace it on the floor. You will notice that as you move through this pattern, changes in direction are already taking place. Trace your pathway again on the floor, and this time try changing levels. Attempt to remember where you have made the level changes. Do the same thing with focus and the size of body movement so that these two aspects of space also change as you move through the same floor pattern. Next try changing two of the aspects of space such as

Figure 3.3

Different ways of placing the arms and body also change the way movement looks. Photo courtesy of Jim Wanner.

level and focus at the same time or on the same beat in the pattern.

Another interesting spatial variation is to add arm movements to your floor pattern. As you experiment with movement variation, you will discover that the arms can make many different patterns in space as the feet and legs continue to trace the same pathway using the same *locomotor* steps. Changes can also be made in the position of the body. Try curving the body forward from the waist, arching the upper back, or even tilting the torso to the side as you move through the same floor pattern (Figure 3.3). You could even perform this same combination of movements backwards, starting at the end and progressing to the beginning. Decide which variation or variations on the floor pattern you find most appealing.

Time.   It is possible to play with variations in the timing of the same floor pattern. Manipulation of *tempo* is easier, however, if you are moving with a basic underlying sound or pulse. Once the beat is established, you can try moving faster or more slowly as you go through the same pattern. You will find that some movements can be done faster, while others cannot be performed skillfully at a more rapid speed.

Another variation could be to put an emphasis or *ac-*

cent on certain steps or actions in the pattern (Hawkins, 1964). Place these accents on different counts during the performance of the entire pattern and then select the use of accents that works best. You can also insert *silences* in your movement pattern, continuing the combination after each silence. You will find new movement patterns taking shape as you experiment with changes of tempo or with the addition of accents and silences. Compare the new pattern with the original.

The manipulation of movement can be used in aerobics routines. Familiar steps and movements can be varied in terms of direction, size, or level. It is not necessary to do all steps forward, backward, or in place. Steps can be easily executed in a circle or even in a figure 8. Actions can also be changed by adding a different use of visual focus or by using the arms in another spatial pattern. Such variations are fun to learn and frequently test coordination at the same time. Changes in timing also add interest. For example, participants enjoy doing a step or action and then repeating the same step or action in double time, or twice as fast as it was performed originally.

Dance energies. There are six basic ways to channel *energy* in dance. These six ways of using energy to propel your actions are known as movement *qualities* and include sustained, percussive, vibratory, swinging, suspended, and collapsing actions. To *sustain* movement is to move slowly, continuously, and with control. Sustained movement can be stopped at any point during the action; it has the appearance of an individual moving in a slow motion film. In contrast to sustained movement, *percussive* action creates direct lines in space and is explosive or sharp. *Vibratory* movement, as its name suggests, consists of trembling or shaking. Trembling actions can be done with one part of the body, such as an arm or a leg, or with the entire body.

Swinging movement traces an arc or curved line in space. When performing swinging movement, you must allow your body to relax and give in to gravity on the downward part of the motion. Energy must then be applied on the upward part of the arc or swing. Like vibratory motion, swinging can be done with one body part or with the whole body by using the torso as the point from which the swinging is initiated. *Suspended* action hovers in space, creating an illusion of defying gravity. The sense of suspension at the highest point of a leap makes suspended action marvelous to observe.

The sixth quality for using energy in movement is *collapsing*. A dancer using collapsing movement is gradually giving in to gravity in a slow descent to the lowest point possible on the floor. Collapsing may be described as a melting or oozing action in a downward direction. It is also possible to do a collapse at a faster speed. The collapse can be done with the whole body as already described or can be performed with just one body part.

You can vary movement through the use of different applications of energy. Pick a series of movement phrases learned in your dance technique class or demonstrated by your teacher. Practice this combination of movements until you have it memorized, and then try changing the movement quality at several points in the combination. Experiment with a number of different uses of energy throughout this series, selecting these variations from sustained, percussive, vibratory, swinging, suspended or, collapsing energy qualities. Notice how changes in quality affect the use of space and timing throughout the same pattern.

Variation in energy can also apply to aerobics. To perform all movements with the same quality is very monotonous. Although the vigorous nature of the actions is of primary importance to aerobics routines, some variation in the use of energy is possible. Use of energy should complement the musical accompaniment as well.

Shapes. As you move, your body can take on many *shapes.* Your body's ability to assume different shapes can provide you with another way to vary your movement ideas. Some of these body shapes may be rounded, whereas others may be angular or sharp. Practice moving around the dance space and stopping suddenly in an interesting shape. Experiment with many different shapes. Some might be done at a high level, and others could be low. These shapes could also be expansive or narrow in the area surrounding your body.

Let your body assume a shape. Concentrate on how this shape feels. Use a full length mirror to study a series of shapes that you can make with your body. Relate a shape that you can make with your body to a shape made by another person. Move with this person, allowing the shapes formed by both of your bodies to intertwine in space. Select a sequence of different shapes, and provide transitional movements from one group of shapes to the next. Try to remember the sequence of groupings and transitions that you just improvised so that you and your partner are able to do them again.

Movement and communication

As indicated in chapter 1, communication through movement is sometimes the goal of a piece of choreography. At other times, a desire for expression is not the intent; sometimes the choreographer seeks to design a composition emphasizing movement alone. In the latter type of dance, frequently the goal is to experiment with variations of each phrase, manipulating the movements in terms of space, time, energy, and shape.

Figure 3.4
Various uses of posture project different feelings to the viewer. Photo courtesy of Jim Wanner.

In either case, the movements usually have a message for the audience members. The potential of human movement to communicate is difficult to avoid, even if communication is not the choreographer's intent. We are trained from childhood to recognize certain gestures. Each gesture, we learn, has a message based on our experiences in life. Waving, we discover, is a friendly gesture, whereas a slapping or striking action is interpreted as aggressive or threatening. In her book, Doris Humphrey said that no movement would be made at all without some type of motivation to initiate it (Humphrey, 1959).

Different movements transmit feelings because of the way in which the elements of those movements—space, time, energy, and shape—are used in them (Hawkins, 1964). We have learned to recognize these different uses of the elements of movement through life experience. An expansive use of space, for example, is bold; a small use of space is timid or tentative. When the focus is directed upward, the action has an uplifting effect on the viewer. A downward use of focus indicates sadness or depression. Quick, darting movement portrays urgency or perhaps anger; slow actions evoke tiredness or calmness. A small level of energy suggests weakness; energetic movement appears strong; rounded shapes are graceful or feminine; and angular shapes or groupings are considered masculine.

Figure 3.5

We have learned to read the use of space, time, energy, and shape in gestures such as reaching, waving, or punching. Photo courtesy of Jim Wanner.

When you are out in public, learn to observe the movements of others. This can be a fascinating experience that you may have overlooked. Be aware of the way people carry their bodies and how their posture is organized. Many individuals have postural habits that cause them to tilt their whole bodies forward as they walk. Others lean backward as they move or poke their chins out in front of their bodies (see Figure 3.4). Watch the gestures that people use while communicating with each other. Attempt to relate your observations to the use of space, time, energy, and shape involved in these actions, and learn to look at them in terms of these six elements (see Figure 3.5). Decide how varying the use of these elements causes the movements to have a different feeling. You can keep a notebook of the different actions you see. Human gesture and the movements of natural objects, such as weeds bending in the wind, the motion of ocean waves, or the flickering flames of a fire, can provide movement ideas from which a dance can be developed.

Use of stage space

When viewed by the audience, an empty stage is a vast expanse of open space. The choreographer's job is to design movement in order to bring this space to life. The stage is dead space until a dancer moves

Figure 3.6

The dancer in the center appears largest and attracts the most attention. The downstage dancer projects intimacy, while the two upstage dancers to the right and left are more remote from the audience. Photo courtesy of Jim Wanner.

through and around it (Hawkins, 1964). Watch someone move through a space in front of you and notice how that space becomes energized. Have this same person stand in one spot and move his or her arms and legs in different directions. Again you will see how the sphere or area surrounding his or her body comes alive.

Once the choreographer has found appropriate movements that suit the intent of the dance and has worked with manipulating and varying these movements, then it is time to set the choreography. Setting a composition involves several steps. First the choreographer must decide on an order for selected actions. Then which actions each dancer is to perform must be determined. Next it is necessary to place and move the dancers around the stage space. Finally, the choreographer needs to select interesting groupings for and relationships between dancers so that the total picture created is well-proportioned. A dancer advancing toward the audience is moving *downstage*. To retreat in the opposite direction, away from the audience, is to go *upstage*. Movement to the side is to *stage right* or to *stage left* according to the performer's right or left side.

The stage is divided into a number of areas that differ in relative importance to the audience; movements per-

Figure 3.7a

An example of poor blocking. Photo courtesy of Jim Wanner.

Figure 3.7b

The appearance of a group of dancers is improved with better spacing. Photo courtesy of Jim Wanner.

formed in each of these stage areas have varying impacts. Dancing center stage attracts the most attention, and a soloist or lead dancer should perform center stage (Humphrey, 1959). Movement done upstage appears remote or mysterious, whereas downstage action is much more intimate and is often reserved for comedy (Humphrey, 1959). The areas at the side to stage right or left are weaker (see Figure 3.6).

Various *pathways* on stage also differ in terms of importance to the audience. Movement executed in straight lines is seen as strong and direct. It is very powerful, for example, to advance from an upstage position directly downstage toward the audience; this pathway is straight and direct, and the dancer becomes progressively larger (Ellfeldt, 1967). Movement done on the diagonal pathways from upstage to downstage corners is also powerful (Ellfeldt, 1967). Curved pathways lack the strength of movement performed in straight lines. When an individual follows a curved pathway, his facing changes constantly and the impression left with the audience is less forceful.

Placing dancers in a stage area and moving them from one stage area to another is known as *blocking* a dance. When you work with groups of several dancers,

Figure 3.8

These two dancers are seen separately rather than as part of one group. Photo courtesy of Jim Wanner.

Figure 3.9a

An example of poor use of facing, hiding the overall shape of the movement. Photo courtesy of Jim Wanner.

do not place the downstage performers directly in front of those who are upstage. It works choreographically to have dancers overlapping in the visual space, but there is no reason to place an individual upstage if a downstage performer completely blocks him from the audience (see Figures 3.7a and 3.7b). On the other hand, do not position dancers in extreme stage right and left positions when you want them both to be seen as part of one *ensemble*. This placement of performers divides audience attention; it is impossible to focus on either dancer for any length of time (see Figure 3.8).

The direction dancers *face* while performing movement is equally important. They should be instructed to face in a direction that allows action to be viewed to the greatest advantage. Do not face a performer in a direction in which part of the performed movement is hidden or that is not complementary to the dancer (Humphrey, 1959). Arm or leg movements executed in front of the body, for example, cannot be seen when the dancer is facing upstage. An arabesque performed with the body facing directly toward the audience is not totally visible either. A diagonal or side facing should be used for an arabesque instead. In addition,

Figure 3.9b

Improved facing. Photo courtesy of Jim Wanner.

Figure 3.9c

A complementary facing on the diagonal for an arabesque. Photo courtesy of Jim Wanner.

diagonal facings are often a much more pleasing way to view a dancer's body than facings from the front or back (see Figures 3.9a, 3.9b, and 3.9c). Take care in placing dancers in ways that could be offensive to the audience. Positions on the floor with the seat toward the audience, for example, can disturb some people. Use your discretion here.

The performer's facial expression may also be important to the intent of a choreography. Consider your dancers' faces when positioning them in the stage space; facial expressions can enhance the audience appeal of your work (Humphrey, 1959). The impassive face is appropriate only for choreography in which the intent is to be devoid of feelings or messages (Humphrey, 1959).

Occasionally, there is a need to choreograph a *dance in the round*. Dance in the round can be very interesting and presents numerous possibilities. However, dance in the round makes the choreographer's job more complex because the performers are viewed from all directions. The use of blocking, facing, and direction must be carefully considered from all perspectives (Ellfeldt, 1967).

Figure 3.10a

A symmetrical shape with one dancer.
Photo courtesy of Jim Wanner.

Figure 3.10b

Tilting the previous shape slightly causes
it to become asymmetrical. Photo courtesy
of Jim Wanner.

Figure 3.10c

An asymmetrical shape. Photo courtesy of
Jim Wanner.

Figure 3.10d

Another asymmetrical shape.
Photo courtesy of Jim Wanner.

Dancers go through many different groupings as they perform a piece of choreography. These groupings are created by the way the choreographer has designed the spatial relationships between dancers. Spatial groupings can be dull, or they can be interesting to the eye and add much to the composition's audience appeal.

The shape a single dancer makes with his or her body can appear balanced or unbalanced to the eye.

Figure 3.11a

A symmetrical grouping of three dancers. Photo courtesy of Jim Wanner.

Figure 3.11b

An asymmetrical grouping with more than one individual. Photo courtesy of Jim Wanner.

When a shape is balanced, the right side of the body mirrors the left side. Such balanced shapes are *symmetrical* (Humphrey, 1959). *Asymmetrical* shapes are unbalanced from the right to the left side of the body and tend to be off-center and more exciting to watch (Humphrey, 1959). (See Figures 3.10a, 3.10b, 3.10c, and 3.10d.) An entire grouping of dancers can create an overall shape that is symmetrical or asymmetrical as well. When viewing such groupings, it is necessary to see the total picture created by the dancers rather than focusing on one or two dancers in the group (see Figures 3.11a and 3.11b). It is also necessary that the choreographer see such groupings as dynamic, not static. The essence of dance is motion, not a stagnant positioning of performers. If dancers do hold a grouping, it is important that the grouping be interesting to look at and that the individuals in the grouping retain a sense of energy and liveliness.

You can practice grouping dancers. Try forming several symmetrical groupings, and then position dancers in several groupings that are asymmetrical. If performers are well-placed, your eye travels comfortably around the whole arrangement of dancers. The grouping should also have a *focal point* (see Figure

Figure 3.12

Another asymmetrical grouping. Notice how your eye focuses first on the dancer on the left, travels along the female dancer's arm, and then focuses on the right-hand dancer. A focal point for the whole design is located at the waistline of the middle dancer. Photo courtesy of Jim Wanner.

3.12). Also look at the kind of lines that are created in space with the performer's arms and legs. It is better to group together individuals who all make straight lines or who all make curved lines with their bodies. Mixing curved and straight lines together in one grouping usually does not work.

Next try adding movement to your groupings. Have your dancers move around the space while retaining a particular grouping. Then have them move through a grouping rather than stopping and holding it in place. Next have your dancers make transitional movements from one grouping to another. These transitions can consist of movement pathways that take them directly from one grouping to another, or they can be indirect pathways that take the performers out into space and then back together again into the next arrangement.

Dancers relate in both space and time throughout a single piece of choreography. The way performers relate in time must be carefully designed. One way to arrange your dancers with respect to timing is to have them all doing the same movements at the same time. This method of choreographic design is known as *unison* movement (Hayes, 1955). Unison movement can be strong and powerful, but it is boring when used repeatedly in a composition. Another technique to set the timing in a piece is to have the dancers begin movement sequences on different counts. Dancer number one, for example, might begin moving on count one of a sequence, while the second and third dancers in

Figure 3.13

An example of sequential movement design. Photo courtesy of Jim Wanner.

Figure 3.14a

Use of opposition. Notice the space between the dancers as well as the area surrounding them. Photo courtesy of Jim Wanner.

Figure 3.14b

Opposition facing on the diagonal. Photo courtesy of Jim Wanner.

the ensemble start dancing on count four. Such an arrangement, known as *sequential* movement, creates an overlapping effect; movements are seen once and are then seen again several counts later (Hayes, 1955). Sequential movement can be created by having dancers enter the stage at different times or by stopping the action in a grouping, having the individuals begin movement again on different counts (see Figure 3.13).

A third method for arranging movement involves an understanding of both space and time. It is called *opposition* in choreographic terms. Opposition means that the dancers move in opposite directions in space. It can be developed from unison movement or from sequential actions (Humphrey, 1959). In opposition, the performers can move from one side of the stage to

Figure 3.15

Steve Paxton in Backwater Two-some, *1978. Photograph by Stephen Petegorsky, Northhampton, MA, courtesy of the Dance Collection, the New York Public Library at Lincoln Center.*

another, or they can travel diagonally between upstage and downstage corners, crossing over in space or moving between each other. Opposition in composition creates an effect in which the space between and surrounding the dancers seems to narrow and widen as they travel across it (see Figures 3.14a and 3.14b).

Choreographic ideas from the avant-garde

The dance world has experienced many new choreographic forms and ideas in the last 20 years. Some of these experimental dance forms have remained, and others have vanished.

One *avant-garde* method of choreography, known as dance by chance, has already been described. You can use dance by chance as part of your choreographic technique. Hand out several different pieces of paper with movement descriptions on them to each of several dancers. Let each individual practice the phrases, and then arbitrarily designate which phrases each dancer is to perform. Other variations would be to change the count on which each dancer begins his or her phrase or to have your dancers begin their series of movements from different points in the stage space. Next try different pieces of music with the same movements.

Figure 3.16

Meredith Monk/The House *at Goddard College, 1972. Photograph by Monica Moseley, courtesy of the Dance Collection, the New York Public Library at Lincoln Center.*

The use of *pedestrian* movement or everyday movement is another device used in some experimental choreography. In *Proxy,* Steve Paxton created a 16-minute work for three dancers. Walking, carrying, and standing were included among the movements in this piece; in addition, the dancers drank a glass of liquid and ate a piece of fruit (McDonagh, 1970) (see Figure 3.15).

You can experiment with pedestrian movements. Select a combination of dance movements, and then interject some action of a pedestrian nature at intervals in this sequence. Choreograph several different sequences in which such pedestrian actions are used. Be aware of the transitions you have used between dance movement and pedestrian action.

Experimental choreographers have often danced in unusual environments such as on the altar of a church, out in the street, or inside an art museum. Meredith Monk, another experimentalist, enjoyed doing works that depended on their placement in different environments. At Woodstock she did a piece in two brick buildings that faced each other. The first part of this composition was done in a space on the ground floor of one of the buildings. The audience then moved outside to watch the dancers appear in the windows of the facing building; the work was concluded by a performer on the roof (McDonagh, 1970). (See Figure 3.16.)

Figure 3.17

Many different kinds of props and objects can be used to create a change in the studio environment for improvisation. Photo courtesy of Jim Wanner.

The use of different settings other than a stage can increase stimulus for the creation of dance movement. On a warm day, take your dance group or class out on the lawn and structure an improvisation in which the dancers are encouraged to move in relation to the objects in this new setting. Check your campus or dance building for other spaces that could provide an altered environment for improvisations. Creating an experimental environment in your customary dance space is also fun. Props such as hoops, chairs, boxes, and scooters can be placed or suspended at points around the room. Other props, such as a screen or the piano, are large enough for individuals to hide behind. Allow your dancers to do movements that can be performed around, over, under, through, behind, or partially inside the props provided. Remind the performers to react and move in relation to each other as well as to the props (see Figure 3.17). After the improvisation has continued for a while, select some of the most effective sequences and set them in a study.

The use of improvisational performance is another interesting choreographic device that has developed along with other avant-garde ideas. The improvised dance composition is based on a *structured improvisation.* Here, certain criteria for movement and manipulation of dancers are set forth. These criteria then direct the dancers' actions in terms of where and how they will move in the performance space. Elements of chance are also involved in a structured improvisation, but to a lesser degree than their use in dances developed by chance.

An example of a structured improvisation is a piece in which the dancers are instructed to move in a circular and counterclockwise pathway, using only walking, running, crawling, and standing or silences. The dancers are also told to be sensitive to each other, picking up the movement of other individuals when it feels right (Dilley, 1981). Another structured improvisation could be based on spatial corridors. In this improvisation, the individuals are told that they can move across the room in several selected columns of the dance space. Again the kinds of movement with which dancers traverse the space is prescribed, and, if a dancer crosses the entire space and reaches the other side of the room, he or she can reenter only by exiting on his side of the dance space and entering again by way of a different corridor (Dilley, 1981).

Contact improvisation is another creative movement idea that has emerged in recent years. Like some other experimental dance ideas, contact improvisation is used both creatively in the studio and as a performance medium. Contact work is a spontaneous form drawn from functional actions performed while relating to the environment or to a moving partner (Brown, 1980). Motivation is taken from one's reactions to being in contact with another moving body or bodies; dancers learn to take and receive impulses from each other. The point of contact between two bodies or between several bodies is not predetermined but is allowed to evolve and progress naturally. Often the weight of one dancer's body is supported by another. Sessions in contact improvisation should be conducted with care. Participants must be instructed in efficient movement techniques. They should know how to relax when falling, roll when meeting the floor, bear weight safely, and catch themselves protectively and yet be able to keep the energy going (Brown, 1980). In contact improvisation, one is able to watch "the ever changing forms of the human body as it falls, supports, jumps, catches, lifts, and follows another body. This quality of functional grace is shared with most sports" (Brown, 1980, p.7).

Looking at the total picture

When you choreograph a dance, you must learn to look at the total picture that your work creates. Spatially, the dancers form groupings at any single point in time. Each of these groupings must be dynamic and not static, creating an interesting picture for the eye.

Your choreography also creates a series of pictures through time; one part of your dance should lead naturally into the next section with good transition between the two. Such transitions are necessary so that the whole piece develops and has a continuous form through time.

As you observe your choreography, imagine it to be enclosed in a picture frame. If you are watching your dance on stage, the picture frame is already in place in terms of the *proscenium* arch surrounding the stage. Your dancers are the colors, lines, and figures in your painting. Notice whether or not they all fit together to comprise a total picture. Be aware of the space between and around your dancers because this space is also part of the total picture you are creating. At times the space between dancers will appear to be moving as if it had a life and movement of its own; it actually becomes part of the motion of the dance. This effect is one about which many dance critics have deliberated. The effect of moving space is an illusion created by the performers' ability to throw energy out into space as they move through it. Suzanne Langer, the famous philosopher, once described the illusions created in a dance as not being real but rather comprising a *virtual* entity that is greater than the actual physical components of human bodies in motion (Langer, 1957). In other words, the choreographer creates a magical entity for the audience—an entity that consists of many separate movements and shapes but that, in a successful piece of choreography, forms a whole from beginning to end. It is important that you learn to think of your choreography in terms of a whole and that you keep this whole in mind when working on any part of the entire work (Hawkins, 1964).

Coaching your dancers

You can begin teaching your movement to dancers once you have found some phrases through improvisation, have worked with varying these phrases, and have an idea for the development of your work. You may find that the dancers perform your movements exactly as you visualized, although this is usually not the case. In designing most compositions, the choreographer has to nurture the execution of the movements by carefully coaching the dancers to get them to perform the work as it was imagined and conceived.

Projection is one aspect of performing that requires coaching. If a dance is to reach an audience, it must *project*. Dancers must perform with sensitivity and awareness; they must learn to direct their energies toward the audience. To aid projection, suggest that your dancers breathe with their movement and that they allow their energy to flow freely between body center and extremities. To help your dancers learn to project, encourage them to reach and stretch and to focus outward while moving.

Communicating with your dancers about the intent of your choreography can significantly enhance performance level. Such communication enables performers to get involved in the motivation of the composition and to understand your ideas. Appropriate imagery can be a helpful coaching tool here. Try to think of as many images as you can that relate to ideas behind your choreography, and keep these images in mind as you work. Describe some of these mental pictures to your dancers when a problem arises concerning the performance of a particular movement or movements. If one image does not connect, try another. Be persistent and creative in coaching your performers, and do not give up until the execution fits your intent.

When you have finished choreographing and coaching, take time to observe the performance of your dance. A videotape of the presentation can be an appropriate learning aid at this point. If you have access to quality color videotape equipment, use it. Any videotape machine, even one that produces a black and white copy, is helpful. Make a video of the entire choreography, and have the performers watch it immediately. You can point out specific performance problems as the tape is reviewed, but the dancers themselves will notice points at which they have done movements incorrectly. One viewing of a tape usually produces marked improvement in performance quality. Videotapes also provide an excellent method of keeping records of each of your choreographies. Store them in a dry, cool place away from heat, light, or electromagnetic sources such as a television, loudspeaker, or microwave oven.

The critique

As you learn to choreograph, you will put together many dance studies. Your teachers will select appropriate motivation for these studies and will guide you through the steps of development. Listen carefully to their suggestions about your work, and relate these suggestions to your developing knowledge of the choreographic craft. Try not to take evaluations in a negative way. Remember that improvement comes gradually and that a critique of your choreography is not a critique of you as an individual but of your composition or study. Creating artistic work can be intensely personal, and it is sometimes difficult to interpret evaluation constructively as positive input unless you earnestly concentrate on doing so. A critique of one's work in creative movement must be interpreted and utilized objectively and should not be seen as criticism of you as a person.

Suite Romance *by Karen Genoff Campbell. Photo courtesy of Bill Scherer.*

The Finished Product: The Performance

Whether you are presenting an informal or formal dance concert, it is wise to plan the content of your performance carefully. Program content should thus be based on the interests and needs of the dance audience in your school and community (Hayes, 1955). It is helpful to include some explanatory material in your program if you are living in a community where dance is not well-known (Hayes, 1955). Such explanatory programs serve to educate the audience and usually take the form of a *lecture-demonstration* on dance content or choreographic principles. The format of a lecture-demonstration involves you or someone else who presents verbal material on dance. The lecture portion of the program is accompanied by dance movement related to the explanation. Your whole production could be a lecture-demonstration, or the demonstration format might be combined with a short concert. A community that is knowledgeable about dance would be able to appreciate a dance concert without the aid of explanatory materials (Hayes, 1955).

Program content should also be planned to suit the tastes prevalent in an area. It would not be wise, for example, to produce an experimental dance concert in a conservative community. You will not build an audience for your programs unless you attempt to connect with the needs and ideas of the audience. Some experimental works can be included later after your concerts have gained a following.

Program variety is also necessary. In planning a dance concert, you must try to include works of different styles so that the program has variety, particularly with respect to group size and choreographic style. Do not place all the solos or all the large-group pieces one after another in the concert, and make sure that you alternate the order of light and serious compositions. (Ellfeldt & Carnes, 1971). The dance presented immediately before intermission should be entertaining in tone to make the audience want to come back for the second part of your show. It is also an excellent idea to save the best for last. This way the concert has a feeling of building in energy toward the end.

Program order should be based on both practical and aesthetic considerations. It may be necessary to have some quick costume changes when the same dancer or dancers perform in one piece right after another. Try to accomplish these costume changes as rapidly and smoothly as possible. If you are able to arrange your concert to avoid quick costume changes, do so.

Once a dance is choreographed and the movement is set, a considerable amount of finishing needs to be done. Some of this polishing is done by proper coaching of the dancers, but presentation of the final product requires going through several other steps including (a) recording the music; (b) designing and executing the costumes; and (c) planning the lighting. The rehearsals, including blocking, technical, and dress rehearsals, are also part of the final stages of dance concert production.

Preparing the accompaniment

Ideally, accompaniment for dance should be live. This is true of both classroom accompaniment and accompaniment for dance performances. Live accompaniment provides better quality and greater flexibility than recorded sound, but the cost of paying musicians is usually excessive for most dance programs or studios.

The goal when using recorded music is to achieve sound of the highest quality possible. To do this, new records should be used for the *master tape*. Old records are likely to produce sound that has many pops and cracks, and extraneous sounds are magnified when reproduced over a loudspeaker system. High-quality audio tapes should be used to produce the master tapes for a performance. Always make a copy of your master tape and have it available during the presentation for emergency purposes. Extra tape recorders should also be on hand for a show.

When recording your master tapes, splice a light-colored leader between the accompaniment for each work. This will allow you and your audio technician to see where you have stopped the tape and to stop only at a point between accompaniments for specific dances. It is a good idea to write the name of each choreography on the tape leader preceding it to prevent mistakes in pausing the tape in the sequence of the concert. Labeling each piece also enables you to cope with last minute emergencies such as the need to delete a dance from the program. All recording should be done at a uniform audio level loud enough to be heard throughout the theater. The use of different audio levels from one dance to the next requires constant adjustments in volume throughout the concert. Audio cassettes can be used for the master tape, but they present more problems in terms of locating specific points on the recording.

The audio technician should be included at rehearsals because the technician needs to learn the sequence of movements that make up each composition. The person operating the sound sytem should take notes concerning movement *cues* related to changes in accompaniment. Sound cues include changing volume, fading sound in or out, and turning accompaniment on or off.

Figure 4.1

Unitards put together with brightly colored wigs and leg warmers create simple but comical costumes.
Future Groove *choreographed by Kay Carara. Photo courtesy of Bill Scherer.*

Check the speakers to be used during the performance. If they produce poor-quality sound, try to replace them with better equipment. When possible, use a stereo rather than monaural sound system and ensure that the accompaniment can be heard both onstage by the dancers and by the audience in the theater. It is sometimes necessary to place a portable speaker on each side of the stage to provide adequate sound for the performers.

Costuming the dance

One of the first rules of dance costuming is to ensure that the costumes complement the choreography, not distract from it. A dance costume should enhance the movement of a choreography, not hide it. The most effective costumes are simple in design. You have defeated your purpose if the audience focuses on costumes rather than movement.

The costumes for a dance should be developed from the same idea or ideas that motivated the creation of the choreography itself. As you consider costume sug-

Figure 4.2

Here unitards provide costuming for a more serious dance. The Guarded Soul *choreographed by Dale Lee Niven-Cooper. Photo courtesy of Bill Scherer.*

Figure 4.3

A costume from a period in American history. Doris Humphrey (center) in her choreography The Shakers. *An uncredited photograph courtesy of the Dance Collection, the New York Public Library at Lincoln Center.*

gestions, review the feeling, intent, or style that you were trying to create in your piece. Clarify this intent and keep it in mind while you are deciding on appropriate costumes. There are several relevant points to consider with respect to dance costumes: (a) style or cut of the garments, (b) costume color or colors, and (c) flow and weight of materials.

Costume style can aid in creating choreographic mood. In Figure 4.1, the costumes indicate a playful and comic mood, whereas in Figure 4.2 the costumes project a more serious mood. The costumes in Figure 4.3 place the dance in a specific historical period.

Costume color also plays a major role in setting the feeling of a piece. Colors such as red, yellow, brown, orange, pink, or rose are considered warm, and green, blue, gray, purple, lavender, or black are cool. You must think of your dancers when selecting costumes. Consider their skin colorings, body builds, and respective heights; choose costume colors that are complementary to your dancers' hair and skin color, and remember that heavy dancers appear more slender

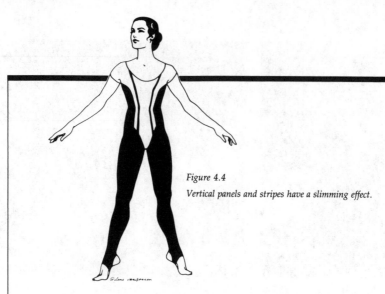

Figure 4.4
Vertical panels and stripes have a slimming effect.

when clothed in darker colors. Lighter or more brightly colored costumes should be used for dancers without weight problems. If it is necessary to costume a heavy dancer in a light or brightly colored costume, select costumes that camouflage wide hips or other figure problems. This can be done by adding stripes or patches of a darker color in strategic places on a costume (see Figure 4.4).

Sometimes you will have to dye parts of a costume made from white material so that colors match. Dyeing is usually more successful with light shades of a color. Vibrant or deep shades are much more difficult to achieve, and costumes in these shades should be purchased. It is also difficult to dye one part of a costume to match another part that was already the desired color when purchased.

The texture of a material affects the way it will accept a dye. When in doubt, test a swatch of the material in the dye before immersing the entire costume. Synthetic materials generally do not accept dye as well as organic fibers such as cotton. Attempts to remove color from a costume and dye it another hue are usually not successful; a rather gray shade of the desired color usually results. Try not to make mistakes in the dyeing process with the hope of removing dyes and starting over with another color for that same garment.

Skillful use of costuming can enhance the effect of

Figure 4.5a

Group unity and design are heightened through use of the same color costumes. Photo courtesy of Jim Wanner.

Figure 4.5b

There is a tendency to focus individually on each of the dancers in a group when they are costumed differently. Photo courtesy of Jim Wanner.

Figure 4.5c

The use of a lighter color leotard and tights calls attention to the downstage dancer. Photo courtesy of Jim Wanner.

a grouping of dancers. Unity can be heightened through knowledgeable use of costume color and style, even though individual dancers in a work are of different heights and body structures. Dressing all dancers in one color creates unity (see Figure 4.5a). A more interesting effect can be created by using one or two shades of the same color within a group. Here unity is maintained, but the stage space has greater depth and appears more interesting to the eye. Placing each performer in a group in a different color or in a different style garment destroys harmony by causing the audience to focus separately on each dancer (see Figure 4.5b). If possible, the soloist should be dressed in a

style or color different than the other performers (see Figure 4.5c). Avoid the use of large bold prints, plaids, and stripes because they tend to distract the audience from focusing on the dance.

Go to a fabric store when you are ready to select materials for dance costumes. When you find a material in the right color, unwind some of it from the bolt. Move the material around to see how it flows. Stiff materials stand away from the body and hide and inhibit an individual's movements; select material that flows *with* a performer's actions. If possible, test a material by draping some of it on one of your dancers and watching the dancer move in it. The weight of a material is also important. Very light-weight materials, such as nylon chiffon, create a floating effect when a performer moves. Materials that have more body, such as jersey, flow with the dancer but cling more closely to the body.

You can extend and vary movement in a choreography through proper use of costuming. A long, flowing skirt can heighten the effect of actions performed with the legs, and the choreographer can even use a skirt to help find movements for a work during the improvisational process. A flowing cape or long, flowing sleeves on a costume can also be used to enhance

Figure 4.6b

A costume with horizontal panels or stripes would not be appropriate for a short, stocky dancer.

Figure 4.6c

This leotard could not be adapted easily for use in later performances.

a dance, and fabrics that stretch easily can become part of the choreography (see Figures 2.1, 2.5, and 2.6).

A basic *leotard* is the best costume for most student performances. It is a good idea to have a stock of plain leotards in many different colors. These leotards can then be paired with *tights* of the same or a contrasting color for use in various concerts. Sleeves, collars, tops, pants, or skirts can be added to a leotard or to the combination of a leotard and tights to create a more detailed appearance. Leotards in unusual colors or of unusual design cannot be adapted as readily for use in later performances.

Figures 4.6a and 4.6b illustrate examples of poorly designed dance costumes. In Figure 4.6a, the costume is too intricate and would divert attention away from the choreography. This costume would also inhibit

Figure 4.7a

A simple bow with clean lines. Photo courtesy of Jim Wanner.

movement and get in the way of the performance. The garments shown in Figure 4.6b cut the body horizontally, making the dancer appear short and stocky rather than tall and lean. Figure 4.6c is representative of a leotard that could not be adapted for use in many separate concerts.

The *unitard* or body suit has become a popular dance costume in recent years. Unitards are made in one piece to cover the entire body. Decorations can be added to them, and they are available in styles with or without sleeves and with various necklines. Unitards are made of an elasticized material that fits the body closely so that they are not complementary to heavy dancers. A unitard is about as expensive as a pair of tights and a leotard together but is not as versatile (see Figure 4.2).

Mounting the dance on stage

You will have rehearsed your dance many times in a studio or gymnasium before bringing it to the theater. When you first begin to *mount* your dance onstage during the blocking rehearsal, have the dancers run through the entire piece. As you do this, decide where you need to position some of the dancers. The placement and positioning of dancers onstage is known as a *blocking rehearsal*. Be clear about the floor patterns to be followed by each dancer throughout the progression of the piece. You should also indicate how per-

Figure 4.7b

A bow that is too elaborate and distracting. Photo courtesy of Jim Wanner.

formers are to relate to each other in the stage space, and entrance and exit points should be clearly indicated to each dancer. As a safety precaution, be sure to clarify the position of all technical equipment that will occupy space onstage and in wing areas. The dancers must know the placement of all masking, wiring, and lighting equipment so that there are no dangerous surprises during the program! All loose wires should be taped down, and rugs should be placed over sharp or protruding equipment to prevent injury. Warn dancers about *sight lines*. Performers should not be visible until they are part of the action onstage. A good rule here is to stand very close to and behind the *leg* or side curtain when awaiting an entrance onstage. Generally, if a dancer can see members of the audience from where he or she is standing, then these audience members can probably see the dancer, too.

In some concerts you might be able to close the front curtain after each dance. In other theaters this may be too time consuming, and it is advisable to have dancers enter the darkened stage with the front curtain open. If this is the case, stage entrances should be made in a calm and collected manner. The dancers will find their starting positions more easily if the stage floor is marked with fluorescent tape.

It is customary to have the performers take a bow after a piece is completed. This puts a professional and finishing touch to the choreography. After the dance

Figure 4.7c

A choreographed pose can be used instead of a traditional bow at the conclusion of a dance. A Rhythmic Clue choreographed by Judy Hoffman-Bejarano. Photo courtesy of Bill Scherer.

is ended, the performers should quickly come back onstage. The lights are brought back up, and the dancers take a bow and exit. In most bows, the individuals stand in one line and take a small bow from the waist. The bow should be led by the dancer on the far right or left of the line. A large bow with a flourish of movement down to the floor is not considered in good taste. However, a bow in which the performers assume a pose from the choreography rather than taking a traditional bow can be effective (see Figures 4.7a, 4.7b, and 4.7c).

Lighting the dance

There are two important things to keep in mind when lighting your dance: stage space and lighting direction. The color of the lighting also requires thought and planning.

A larger stage will require more lighting instruments to cover the area. Performers cannot be seen when they dance in the dark, so it is paramount that all important stage areas be illuminated. As a rule, six *pools* of light are sufficient for general lighting of the whole stage (Ellfeldt & Carnes, 1971). The instruments that create these pools are positioned in front of and above the stage floor. The angle of each beam of light is about 45 degrees vertical to the stage floor in order to create the correct shadowing effect on the dancers. This 45-degree angle can be altered to some extent when

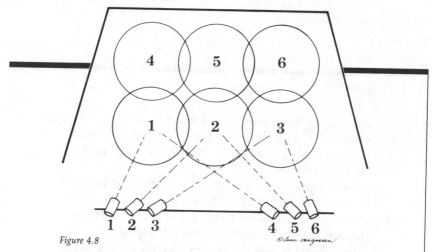

Figure 4.8

The six basic pools of light. Notice how two beams of light come from opposite directions and blend together to create one pool.

conditions do not allow for proper location of lighting instruments. You will have to judge whether or not the desired effect is being achieved. The pools of light must overlap about one foot to alleviate dark spots onstage.

Each pool of light is created by two *spotlights*, one coming from stage right and the other from stage left. Pool or area 1, for example, receives its illumination from spotlights numbered 1 and 4, pool 2 from spotlights 2 and 5, and pool 3 from spotlights 3 and 6 (Ellfeldt & Carnes, 1971) (see Figure 4.8). The lighting instruments used to create these three downstage areas are positioned in the *beams* or are attached to a balcony rail located above the audience and in front of the stage (Ellfeldt & Carnes, 1971). Any instrument that is placed above the audience, however, must be secured according to proper safety regulations. The three upstage areas (pools 4, 5, and 6) then receive their illumination from spotlights placed on a *pipe* closer to the performance area above the *apron* or front of the stage (Ellfeldt & Carnes, 1971).

You should check the dance area for dark spots by having someone walk slowly from one side of the stage to the other while all lighting instruments are on (Ellfeldt & Carnes, 1971). This check should be made without color media on the instruments. Check for dark spots in both upstage and downstage areas. If dark spots exist, add more lighting instruments or adjust the positioning of instruments already in use to make an even effect.

Front lighting has a tendency to flatten the face and body, which makes illumination from the side important in dance. Dance is a very sculptural art form, and the audience must be able to see this aspect of the art. Side lighting molds the dancer's body, adding depth and form to the total picture. To create side lighting, put the instruments on *lighting trees* placed in the *wing* or side positions. These instruments are hidden from the view of the audience by side curtains known as legs. Either spotlights or striplights can be used to create such side lighting. The type of instruments you use will be determined by the number and variety of instruments available. Dark spots can be filled in with additional instruments located in the front positions already described. Providing lighting from both front and side positions is advantageous, but this may not be possible in every situation. In such cases, it is advisable to use the basic general lighting involving six areas or pools. A good rule of thumb is to begin locating lighting instruments so that dancers can at least be seen and then to add any available instruments as needed to give shape and color to the individual dance compositions.

A *cyc* or *cyclorama* provides the background for a dance concert in many cases. A cyc is a large piece of light-colored material that is suspended from a pipe or batten to form the backdrop upstage from the dancers. It is usually curved forward at each end to mask the upstage corners. Lighting instruments are used to throw light on the cyc so that a flood or *wash* of light covers the whole cyc from both above and below the stage. *Striplights* located in front and above the cyc can produce illumination from the top, while ad-

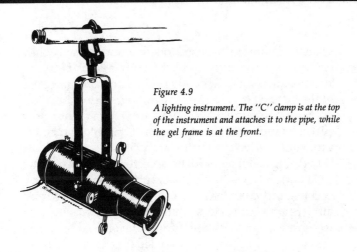

Figure 4.9

A lighting instrument. The "C" clamp is at the top of the instrument and attaches it to the pipe, while the gel frame is at the front.

ditional striplights are laid on the stage floor behind *masking* to create a wash of light from below (Melcer, 1955). Lighting instruments known as *scoops* can also be used to produce a wash of color over the cyc. Sometimes a dark curtain can be an effective background for dance, provided that enough light is still available to illuminate the performers.

Color is created in stage lighting through the use of a medium called *gel*. Gels are manufactured in many different colors and are made of transparent, nonflammable material. Never substitute cellophane for a gel because cellophane burns. A gel changes white light into a color when it is placed in front of the beam of light. The gel is held in place by a frame located at the front of each lighting instrument (see Figure 4.9). The *lamp* in each instrument gives off white light containing all the colors of the spectrum. When a gel is placed in front of white light, it absorbs all the colors out of this white light except the color of the gel itself (Melcer, 1955). When a red gel, for example, is put in front of a beam of light, you will see only red light.

Red, green, and blue are considered the *primary colors* in stage lighting (Melcer, 1955). In general, gels of primary colors are not used to light dance because they are too intense and absorb too much light before it reaches the stage. Gel colors suggested for dance are amber, "bastard" amber, straw, surprise pink, no-color blue, moonlight blue, lavender, frost, and a few pieces of red, green, magenta, and midnight blue for interesting effects (Lippincott, 1956).

Lighting color should be selected to enhance the quality or mood of a choreography. As a rule, blues, greens, and lavenders are cool, and reds, pinks, and ambers are warm colors. Until recently, it was the rule to have warm colors come from one side of the stage and cool colors from the other side, with other colors blended in to heighten the mood. When in doubt about color, follow this rule unless there is a reason, such as the shade of a costume, that you should do otherwise (Melcer, 1955). If you do not have sufficient lighting instruments to create the effect of opposing warms and cools, use a predominance of one color with some of the other colors blended in; never use only one color by itself (Lippincott, 1956). When lighting is done straight on without the appropriate 45 degree angle, it is sometimes better to use a gel that reflects both warm and cool color properties. Such middle-of-the-road colors include special lavender, surprise pink, or chocolate. The primary colors red, blue, and green plus amber (which is not a primary color) can be blended or used alone to create an effective wash on the cyc. Again, color selection must be determined by the mood of a dance and its costuming.

It is essential that you see what all costume colors look like *under the lighting*; putting colored light on a garment can change its color completely. Blue light, for instance, can turn a red costume or red make-up to black, whereas red light on a red costume will intensify its shade (Melcer, 1955). Lighting a dance is much easier if you have used only one or a few differ-

Figure 4.10

A pool of light or special directed from above produces a dramatic effect. Civilized Evil *choreographed by Catherine Wettlaufer. Photo courtesy of Bill Scherer.*

ent costume colors in that number. The best test for selecting lighting color is to have the dancers put on their costumes and move around under the lighting.

Green light and green costumes can be particularly difficult to work with. Green lighting creates an other-worldly effect and should be reserved for dances in which such ambience is desired. Green costumes can be used only under green light because they do not appear to be the proper color under other lighting colors and frequently look muddy as a result.

You can accentuate one or more dancers through the use of special effects. This can be done by directing a more intense spot of light to the point onstage where added audience attention is desired. Such lighting effects to augment general lighting are known as *specials*. A dramatic effect can be achieved by positioning a special directly above the performers' heads so that a pool of light is seen flooding down onto the dancers (see Figure 4.10). Performers should be instructed to head for these specials and to position themselves so that they are in the *hot spot* of the pool of light. Such placement of dancers is especially important during the execution of a lift because the individual being lifted should be illuminated throughout such sequences of movement.

Another kind of special can be created through the use of a *gobo*. A gobo is a special that throws a patterned pool of light on the stage. It can be constructed by cutting the desired pattern in an aluminum pie tin and then placing the tin in front of the light source (Reid, 1982). The pattern cut in the tin is cast in shadow and light on the stage. Gobos can be made to resemble a star-studded sky or the sun filtering through the trees of a forest. The gobo is used only with ellipsoidal spotlights in which it is placed at the gate or perfect center of the instrument. This placement permits the pattern to be projected without distortion. *Do not make gobos out of flammable materials.*

Another interesting lighting technique, although not considered a special, is the use of beams of light directed across the stage from behind some of the dancers' legs. Here, dancers' bodies are flooded in light as they pass through each beam between upstage and downstage areas. Silhouette and shadow can also enhance the impression created in a choreography.

A *followspot* is very commercial looking, but if available it can call attention to an individual dancer. The followspot is operated by a technician and is usually located in the light booth at the back of the theater. When used in a gymnasium setting, it is placed above and behind the audience. Followspots are frequently part of musical theater productions or ice skating shows.

The important point to consider in planning for specials or for other interesting lighting effects is the availability of lighting instruments. You may not have enough lighting instruments to create any of the effects already described. A few extra pieces of equipment, however, can be used for several different specials by changing gel colors or by placing a gobo in front of an instrument. Such changes can be made between dances. Refocusing or changing the placement of lighting equipment should not be attempted during the program because this would slow down the pace of the concert considerably. Dancers may also need to be repositioned to accommodate the use of a limited number of instruments used in specials.

It is an immense help to your technical designer if you are able to put together a rudimentary light plot. Such a light plot should begin with a general description of each dance, particularly a description of the mood or changing moods throughout the pieces (Ellfeldt & Carnes, 1971). Other factors to be included in the general light plot are (a) changes in lighting color (b) costume colors, (c) special effects, (d) placement of props or scenery, and (e) a floor plan of the choreography (Ellfeldt & Carnes, 1971). The complete light plot can then be designed from your description. The final plot is a hanging plot and includes the placement of each instrument, the color with which each instrument is gelled, the circuits connecting instruments to the control panel, and the manner in which instruments are controlled at the panel or *dimmer* board (Ellfeldt & Carnes, 1971).

If you do not have a *technical designer*, you may be able to hire one. You could also enlist the help of a knowledgeable theater student. If you end up doing all of the lighting yourself, keep your design and plot simple. A custodian who works in the theater in which your production will be presented can often familiarize you with the location and operation of equipment.

You will need to conduct a *technical rehearsal* once you have decided on the location and color of your lighting. A technical rehearsal usually follows the blocking rehearsal and gives you or your technicians a chance to practice lighting cues. It also gives the performers an opportunity to become familiar with cues. The dancers may need instructions as to where they should perform certain sections of a choreography so that they are dancing in properly illuminated stage areas. Technicians, particularly those who are not familiar with dance, may need to see a movement several times before they are able to connect it with the appropriate lighting *cue*. In the technical rehearsal, performers mark through an entire piece of choreography. Have the dancers stop at each point where there is a change in the lighting. Later, you or your technicians should practice each lighting change or cue again as a dance is rehearsed. Make sure that you write down each cue, recording the action onstage. Changes in lighting and how to control those changes at the dimmer board should be notated. It may also be necessary to indicate the duration of some lighting changes. Do not trust cues to memory; the number of cues required during a dance performance are far too difficult to memorize. You or your technicians may have to rerun certain segments of a piece until the lighting is done correctly.

Lighting is supposed to be an integral part of a dance performance. Its purpose is to enhance the illusion created by the choreography, not to distract from it. Lighting changes that occur at unplanned points in a dance are disconcerting for both the performers and audience alike. In addition, when a production's lighting is noticed more than its choreography, something is wrong. The intent of choreography is not to design a light show but to blend the two components of dance and lighting together to form a single entity. Since very little scenery is employed in choreography, excellence in lighting is very important.

A word about dance floors

Many stages do not have floor surfaces that are good for dance because the best dance floors are those that are made of a *suspended* wood construction. Theaters that have a cement stage floor are not appropriate and should be avoided if possible.

Check the surface of your stage floor carefully. Look for nails, screws, or other sharp objects that could injure a dancer's feet. Cover splintered areas in the floor with tape. Masking tape works well and can be painted the same color as the floor so it will not be noticed by the audience. Clean the stage floor with a damp mop before each rehearsal and performance to remove dust that could soil costumes.

Today a variety of portable dance floors are commercially available. Most of these floors come in strips of a material similar to linoleum that can be rolled out to cover the stage area to provide a much more ideal dance surface. The separate strips of the *dance floor* are taped in place on stage. A portable floor provides the added advantage that it can be transported from one performance location to another if you decide to take your concert on tour.

Scheduling rehearsals

A well-organized rehearsal schedule is essential for a successful performance. The best way to coordinate a rehearsal schedule is to begin with the day of the concert and move backwards to the time of the first rehearsal in the theater. All rehearsals should be written on a calendar and posted where everyone concerned can check the schedule.

The first set of rehearsals should be for *blocking*. Each choreographer must have a chance to conduct his or her own blocking rehearsal to make sure that the dance is mounted onstage correctly. Portions of time should be set aside for all choreographers to conduct a blocking rehearsal. The suggested time allotment for these rehearsals is about an hour to an hour and a half each, depending on the length of the dance.

Technical or lighting rehearsals follow blocking rehearsals. Again, each choreographer in the concert needs a period of time to view his or her dance as it will appear with lighting, including all the changes in lighting throughout the choreography. Sufficient time should also be set aside for technicians to run through the dance and practice cues. Changes in cues can be made at this time.

Dress rehearsals are run immediately preceding the concert. If there is enough time in the theater, it is advisable to conduct more than one dress rehearsal. Lighting and costumes can be given a final check, and the pace of the entire program can be brought up to speed in the dress rehearsals. Nothing makes an audience more restless than a dance concert with long breaks between each piece. Dancers should be encouraged to make their entrances and exits as quickly and smoothly as possible. Those performers in two or more successive dances should also practice changing costumes quickly. Sometimes the flow of a concert can be accelerated by providing *dressers* for these individuals. The dresser can have a costume change ready when a dancer exits from the stage and can help this performer get into the next costume. A small portable dressing room can be set up behind a screen in the wings of the stage to facilitate quick costume changes.

Informal concerts

In some communities or educational institutions, a stage may not be available for your performance. In such cases, a gymnasium or studio space can be transformed into a relatively professional looking stage for an informal concert.

Illumination can be provided by attaching lighting instruments to volleyball standards or poles using the *"C" clamp* on each instrument (see Figure 4.9). Care should be taken to place instruments so that the lamp inside is positioned correctly. Some lighting equipment

Figure 4.11

Strategically placed flats can give the appearance of
a stage in an informal setting such as a gymnasium.

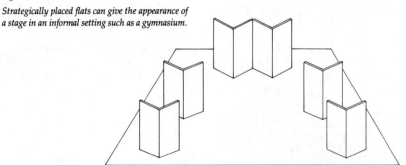

must be burned with the *lamp base* pointed up; other
instruments require the lamp base to be pointed downward; and some lamps can be placed in either a base-
up or a base-down position. Check the instructions for
proper positioning of these instruments. Volleyball
standards with the lighting instruments attached can
then be put in the front and side positions already
described. The important point is that you need to
come up with a performance area that is evenly illuminated. You will have to experiment with the placement of the standards until you obtain the desired
effect. Check each standard for stability before attaching lighting instruments to it. The base of each standard must have enough weight to counterbalance the
heavy instruments. The diameter of the pole of each
standard must also be checked to make sure the clamp
on the lighting instrument will fit around it.

You can mask off or frame the dance space with *flats*
that are easy to build (see Figure 4.11). Flats are constructed by first building a wooden frame. Inexpen-
sive muslin is then stretched over this frame to provide
the surface of the flat (see Figure 4.12a). Two widths
of muslin may have to be double-stitched together to

Figure 4.12a

Back view of two flats held together with loose pin hinges. Notice how the muslin is folded along the edges of the back of the flat and secured in place with staples. Photo courtesy of Jim Wanner.

get a piece of material that is wide enough to cover each flat. The muslin is held in place with staples applied with a gun, and the corners of the muslin are folded under and secured with additional staples. The wood used in the flats should be light in weight because the flats will need to be moved in and out of the storage area for different performances. Generally, 3-1/2 inch by 3/4 inch wood cut in desired lengths is recommended for the construction of flats. Use wood that is not warped and that is thick and strong enough to withstand bending after the muslin is stretched in place. The frame for the flats must be high and wide enough to hide dancers from view while they are waiting to enter the stage area. A frame 5 feet wide by 8 feet high is suggested as the size for each flat.

The flats can be painted once the muslin is stretched over the wooden frames. A water-based paint is recommended; it should not be too thick to spread easily over the surface of the flats. A light colored paint, such as beige, is fairly easy to light; white surfaces appear too stark onstage, and black flats absorb too much light. Beige is a warm color that can be used under many different colors of lighting and that is unlikely to clash with costume colors.

Construct your flats so that they are free-standing;

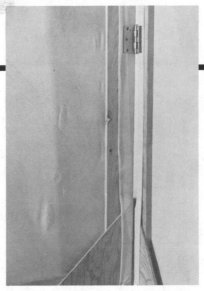

Figure 4.12b

A more detailed photo of the back of a flat showing one of the loose pin hinges. Photo courtesy of Jim Wanner.

flats that need supports behind them to stand take longer to set up. Free-standing flats can be made by putting *loose pin hinges* between each flat. Two flats are then attached together by inserting the pin into each hinge (see Figure 4.12b). These flats can stand without added supports when opened at an angle of less than 180 degrees. They can be placed anywhere in the stage area or used as described earlier to mark off the space in upstage and side positions.

Conclusion

Any creative endeavor is actually an exercise in problem solving. One of the challenges is to choose a direction and then to persevere—to make the imagined a concrete reality. In dance, more than in any of the other arts, there is the potential for creating something from nothing—of molding movement to fit the forms and images emerging from the mind.

The preceding suggestions are offered as a series of steps to follow, particularly in the early stages of choreographic exploration. Hopefully, these suggestions will help with a creative impasse, should one arise, and also provide the reader with many suggestions to release creativity.

Glossary

AB-A simple choreographic form with two sections having two contrasting themes (Blom & Chaplin, 1982).

ABA-Another simple choreographic form including two contrasting themes, A and B, followed by a repeat of the first theme, (Ellfeldt, 1967).

abstract-A dance style without intent to communicate a message. (The word **geometric** is used in this text to avoid confusion with the second meaning of **abstract**-May also refer to the process of presenting the core or essence of the real thing in the work of art.)

abstraction-The process of reducing something to its most basic traits or features (Ellfeldt, 1967).

accent-Providing emphasis or stress on certain musical counts or with specific movements.

alignment-The placement of the body's segments one above the other as closely as possible to a straight line that extends at a right angle to the floor.

apron-The front or downstage portion of the stage.

asymmetrical-An unbalanced body shape or grouping of dancers (Humphrey, 1959).

avant-garde-Recent and experimental developments in the arts.

batten-A metal pipe usually located parallel to the proscenium arch of a stage from which scenery and lighting instruments are hung (Gillette, 1978).

beam-An opening in the ceiling of the theater where lighting instruments are suspended (Gillette, 1978).

blocking-The positioning of dancers onstage after a dance has been choreographed.

canon-A choreographic form usually providing the movement materials for only part of a dance. It is based on the use of one repeated movement phrase performed by different dancers beginning the phrase a number of counts apart (Blom & Chaplin, 1982). The phrases are danced with and against one another.

"C" clamp-The clamp at the top of a lighting instrument by which it is attached to a pipe or batten.

chance-An avant-garde method of choreography based on random methods of selecting movement or random organization of actions to be included in a piece (Bloom & Chaplin, 1982).

character-The basic style, quality, or feeling of a dance or section of a dance.

choreographer-One who finds movement for and organizes actions into dances.

choreography-A whole dance with a beginning, middle, and conclusion.

closure-To bring movement to an appropriate ending, as in the conclusion of an improvisation or the climax of a choreography.

collage-A choreographic form made up of unrelated movements (Blom & Chaplin, 1982).

collapsing-A quality of movement or use of energy described as slowly giving in to gravity.

combination-A grouping of connected movements usually prepared for presentation during the latter portion of a dance technique class. Students are expected to learn and perform combinations as part of the class.

comic-A style of movement that appears funny, odd, or unusual to the viewer.

composition-A dance or choreography that exists as a whole with a beginning, middle, and end.

concert-A program of separate dances performed for the public.

contact improvisation-Spontaneous movement drawn from actions done while relating to the environment or while in contact with another moving body (Brown, 1980).

continuity-A principle of good choreographic form in which there is a natural and organized progression of movement phrases so that one flows naturally into the next (Hawkins, 1964).

contrast-To use different attributes of the elements of movement. High movement contrasts with one done at a low level; fast movement contrasts with slow actions.

count-The number of underlying pulse beats which make up a sequence of movements or a measure of music.

craft-An understanding of how to organize movement into a dance following the discovery of such movements through improvisation; the designing and shaping of a choreography.

cue-The point in a dance at which appropriate changes in lighting or accompaniment need to occur.

cyclorama-A plain piece of cloth extending around and above the upstage area to create a feeling of infinite space and to serve as the background for the dancers (Reid, 1982).

dance-A whole choreography with organization, progression, and development, including a beginning, middle, and end.

dance drama-A choreography expressing a message and involving relationships between the dancer-characters.

dance floor-A portable dance surface usually made of a linoleum-like material that is rolled on the stage in strips and held in place with tape of the same color.

dance in the round-A choreography designed to be viewed from all sides rather than from the front only.

design-A pattern traced in space or on the floor. To organize and structure a piece of choreography.

dimmer-A device that determines the amount of electricity passed to a lighting instrument thereby controlling the brightness of that instrument (Reid, 1982).

direction-One aspect of the movement element space. In dance there are eight basic directions in which a dancer can move or face the body.

downstage-Toward the front of the stage closer to the audience.

dresser-An individual who helps a performer to change costume.

dress rehearsal-The practice or "run through" immediately preceding the performance in which the dancers wear their costumes.

electronic-A type of music from the 20th century lacking customary metric organization and composed by electronic rather than instrumental means.

element-The three basic components of movement—space, time, and energy or force. (Shape is sometimes included as a fourth element.)

energy-One of the elements of movement. Movement is propelled by energy.

ensemble-a group of dancers who perform together.

essence-The fundamental nature of a person or thing.

exploration-Spontaneous movement based on suggestions made by a leader; not as in-depth a process as improvisation (Hawkins, 1964).

facilitator-One who makes suggestions to trigger movement, especially in improvisational situations.

facing-The direction toward which the front of the body is positioned; where one's face is directed.

flat-A wooden frame with muslin stretched over it to provide background and legs in an informal setting.

flow-The transmission of energy from one part of the body to another; the way in which a costume moves in relation to the actions in a dance.

focal point-A place where the audience readily looks on stage or within a group of dancers.

focus-A place where a dancer directs his or her eyes. Also, a point of concentration for the audience.

follow-To copy the movements of another dancer simultaneously.

followspot-A lighting instrument used to highlight and follow a dancer around the stage (Reid, 1982).

force-One of the elements of movement. Force propels movement. (Used interchangeably with the word **energy**.)

form-The overall shape, organization, or development of a choreography.

gel-The media used to give color to white light.

geometric-A dance style with no intent to communicate a message. Its emphasis is on movement variation, line, and design. (The word **abstract** may mean the same thing.)

gobo-A mask placed at the gate of a spotlight to project a pattern with a beam of light by blocking out portions of that light beam (Reid, 1982).

ground bass-A choreographic form, usually providing the movement materials for only part of a dance, in which a phrase or phrases are repeated throughout with a more complex series of movements being played against them by another dancer or dancers (Lockhart, 1982).

hot spot-The most intense place in a pool of light thrown by a spotlight. For good visibility, a dancer should head for the hot spot.

idea-A motif, motivation, or stimulus for movement.

image-A mental picture.

improvisation-Spontaneous movements stemming from a specific stimulus; a more complete and inner motivated movement experience than **exploration** (Hawkins, 1964).

impulse-A burst of energy greater than what came before or after.

informal concert-A program of separate dances performed for the public in an informal setting such as a gymnasium or dance studio.

intent-The motivation behind the creation of a dance.

involvement-Movement experiences requiring more than a superficial level of attention.

isolation-Movements restricted to one area of the body such as the shoulders, rib cage, or hips. Isolations are important in jazz dance.

jazz-A lively energetic dance style that grew from the syncopated rhythms of jazz music. (Kraines & Kan, 1983).

kinesthetic-Relating to the aspects of kinesthesia or the sensation of position, movement, or tension. In this text it also means motivation for movement involving various kinds of actions, sensations of tension, and uses of space.

lamp-The illuminating device within a lighting instrument (Reid, 1982).

lamp base-The bottom of the light source within the instrument. Care must be taken to burn all lamps in the proper position, whether base up or base down.

lecture-demonstration-An informal performance including movement and verbal explanations of aspects of dance.

legs-Curtains at the sides of the stage that hide dancers waiting to enter the performance area.

leotard-A piece of close-fitting dance clothing that covers the body and sometimes the arms.

level-One of the aspects of the movement element space. In dance there are three basic levels: high, middle, and low.

lighting-tree-A vertical, free-standing pipe with side arms to which lighting instruments are attached (Gillette, 1978). Light trees and usually placed in the wings behind the legs.

line-A spatial aspect of dance movement; lines created in space as dancers move, or through the placement of parts of the body in space. Line can be curved or straight.

literal-A kind of choreography that communicates a story or message to the audience (Turner, 1971).

locomotor-Dance movements that cross space.

loose pin hinge-A type of hinge in which the central pin can be easily removed.

lyric-A movement style characterized by actions that are smooth, calm, and controlled.

manipulate-To vary movement, particularly in terms of space, time, energy, or shape.

masking-Neutral materials defining the performance area or concealing technical equipment (Reid, 1982).

master tape-The main original tape recording used to provide accompaniment for a dance concert.

meter-The manner in which music is divided into groupings or measures. Usually each measure has the same number of underlying pulse beats.

mirror-To copy the movements of another while facing that individual.

mixed meter-A musical meter in which the measures differ in terms of the number of underlying pulse beats per measure.

modern dance.-A kind of dancing that evolved at the beginning of the 20th century as contrasted with ballet, tap, or jazz dance. Creative work or choreography is an important part of the learning experience in modern dance.

motivation-The starting point or stimulus for creative movement.

mount-To place and position a dance onstage after the completion of the choreography.

narrative-A choreographic form that tells a story similar to a dance drama (Humphrey, 1959).

nonliteral-Dance that emphasizes movement manipulation and design without the intent of telling a story. Nonliteral works communicate directly without explanations. (Turner, 1971).

opposition-The act of moving or facing the body in opposing directions (Humphrey, 1959).

organic-A dance or sequence of movements that has an interrelationship of parts similar to the form or organization of parts in nature.

overall shape-The form or development of an entire dance or sequence of movements as it progresses from beginning to end.

pantomime-The use of action and gesture without words as a means of expression.

path or pathway-The designs traced on the floor as a dancer travels across space; the designs traced in the air as a dancer moves various body parts.

pattern-The organization of movements into recognizable relationships. (Ellfeldt, 1967). Also refers to the organization of sounds into identifiable groupings.

pedestrian-Movements such as sitting, standing, eating, or typing that are not traditionally done in dance but in daily life.

percussive-A quality of movement or use of energy that is direct, powerful, and explosive.

phrase-The smallest unit of movement in an entire dance (Blom & Chaplin, 1982).

pipe-A long, cylindrical piece of metal usually suspended parallel to the proscenium arch of the stage from which scenery and lighting instruments are hung.

plot-A drawing showing the location of each lighting instrument used in a concert in relation to the physical structure of the theater. May also refer to a general description of lighting changes throughout a choreography.

pool-A circle of light thrown onstage by a lighting instrument. Most pools are actually not a perfect circle due to the location of a lighting instrument and the angle with which the beam of light hits the stage.

primary colors-The three most basic colors in stage lighting, including red, green, and blue. They produce white light when all three are mixed together.

project-To throw one's energy out toward the audience; to make movement on stage more visible; or to be exact in terms of movement expression.

prop-An object that serves as background for a dance; dancers also move on or around a prop or make it a part of the action or spatial design in a choreography.

proscenium-The arch that frames the stage area through which the audience views a dance.

pulse-The underlying and steady beat in dance or music. The pulse is divided into groupings or measures with a specific number of beats per measure; a rhythmic pattern is created over and in relation to the pulse.

quality-Movement characteristics determined by the use of energy (Ellfeldt, 1967).

repetition-A principle of good choreographic form based on using movements or phrases again in a work.

Repetition adds closure; the audience feels familiar and more involved with repeated movements.

rhythm-A structure of patterned movement through time (Ellfeldt, 1967).

rhythmic pattern-The organization of movements or sounds into recognizable groupings or relationships. A rhythmic pattern is created by moving more slowly or faster than the underlying pulse or by leaving silences in the movement (Hawkins, 1964).

rondo-A choreographic form with many different sections in which there is a return to the original theme in alternation with the contrasting sections (Horst & Russell, 1963).

scoop-A lighting instrument primarily used to throw a wash of light on the cyclorama (Gillette, 1978).

section-Part of a dance smaller than the whole that contains many phrases.

semblance-Having the appearance of or resembling something else.

sequence-A series of movements longer than a phrase but much shorter than a section of a dance; similar to a combination.

sequential-An arrangement of movements or phrases producing an overlapping effect in time (Hayes, 1955).

shape-An interesting and interrelated arrangement of body parts of one dancer or group of dancers.

shaping-To give overall form and development to a choreography.

sightline-Lines of visibility onto the stage area from the audience.

silence-An absence of movement in which dancers hold a position.

size-One of the aspects of the movement element space. Size can vary from the smallest possible performance of a movement to the largest.

space-One of the elements of movement. Movement occurs in and crosses space.

special-The use of a pool of light onstage to call attention to or create a particular feeling for a dancer.

spotlight-Any one of a number of types of lighting instruments containing a lens for controlling or condensing a beam of light.

stimulus-The starting point or incentive for creative movement.

striplight-A lighting instrument consisting of 6-8 lamps in a trough; may be mounted vertically or horizontally (Bellman, 1967).

structured improvisation-Spontaneous movement with selection of movement determined by rules set beforehand.

study-A short dance having a beginning, middle, and end that deals with only one or a few aspects of choreography.

style-A personal or characteristic manner of moving or choreographing (Ellfeldt, 1967).

suite-A choreographic form with a moderate first section, second slow section, and lively third part (Humphrey, 1959).

surrealistic-A modern movement in the arts and literature characterized by the representation of dreams or irrational and unusual arrangement of materials.

suspended-A quality of movement or use of energy that gives a feeling of stopping temporarily or hovering in mid-air.

suspended floor-A floor of wooden slat construction that gives with and cushions dance movement, particularly movements where there is landing from elevation.

sustained-A quality of movement or use of energy that is slow, smooth, and controlled.

swinging-A quality of movement or use of energy that traces an arc in space. In a swing, one must relax and give in to gravity on the downward part of the arc and apply energy during the upward action.

symmetrical-A balanced body shape or grouping of dancers (Humphrey, 1959).

syncopate-To place accents where they usually do not occur in the metric organization of both music and dance.

technical designer-One who creates sets and lighting for performers.

technical rehearsal-A performance "run through" during which lighting cues are set in relation to dance movement.

technique-The learning of movement skills; the ability to use choreographic craft.

tempo-The speed of movement as it progresses faster, more slowly, or on a pulse beat (Ellfeldt, 1967).

texture-The structural quality of a dance resulting from the method of using movement.

theme-One or several movement phrases that fit together and are developed from the same idea or intent.

theme and variations-A choreographic form developed from changing a movement theme (Humphrey, 1959).

tights-A close-fitting piece of dance clothing that covers the pelvis, legs, and sometimes the feet.

time-One of the elements of movement. Movement takes place through time.

tone-The quality or feeling in a movement or movements.

transition-A principle of good choreographic form that provides a bridge from one phrase of movement into the next or between sections of a choreography. Transitions should fit into the natural flow of dance movement and not be noticeable (Hawkins, 1964).

unison-To move exactly the same way as others in a group (Hayes, 1955)

unitard-A one-piece, close-fitting dance costume that covers the entire body, including the legs.

unity-A principle of good choreographic form in which phrases fit together with each phrase important to the whole (Hawkins, 1964).

upstage-Toward the back of the stage away from the audience.

variety-A principle of good choreographic form that involves sufficient variation of movement to keep audience interest, while still maintaining unity of the whole (Hawkins, 1964).

vibratory-A quality of movement or use of energy that involves shaking or trembling actions.

virtual-The illusion created in a dance of the work being greater than the separate motions of each individual performer (Langer, 1957).

wash-An even blending of light beams from separate instruments; especially an even flooding of light to cover the cyclorama.

wing-The sides of the stage.

References

Bellman, W. (1967). *Lighting the stage: Art and practice.* Scranton, PA: Chandler.

Blom, L., & Chaplin, L.T. (1982). *The intimate act of choreography.* Pittsburgh: University of Pittsburgh Press.

Brown, B. (1980, Fall). Is contact a small dance? *Contact Quarterly,* p. 7.

Bry, A. (1978). *Visualization: Directing the movies of your mind.* New York: Barnes and Noble.

Dilley, B. (1981, Summer). Notes from improvisation, open structures. Boulder, CO: Naropa Institute.

Dowd, I. (1981, Summer). Notes from alignment of the axial skeleton. Boulder, CO: Naropa Institute.

Ellfeldt, L. (1967). *A primer for choreographers.* Palo Alto, CA: National Press.

Ellfeldt, L., & Carnes, E. (1971). *Dance production handbook or later is too late.* Palo Alto, CA: National Press.

Gillette, M. (1978). *Designing with light.* Palo Alto, CA: Mayfield.

Hanstein, P. (1980, Summer). Notes from improvisation workshop. Denton, TX: Texas Woman's University.

Hawkins, A. (1964). *Creating through dance.* Englewood Cliffs, N.J.: Prentice-Hall.

Hayes, E. (1955). *Dance composition and production.* New York: A.S. Barnes.

Horst, L., & Russell, C. (1963). *Modern dance forms* (2nd ed.). San Francisco: Impulse.

Humphrey, D. (1959). *The art of making dances.* New York: Grove.

Jacobson, E. (1929). *Progressive relaxation.* Chicago: The University of Chicago Press.

Kraines, M.G., & Kan, E. (1983). *Jump into jazz.* Palo Alto, CA: Mayfield.

Langer, S. (1957). *Problems of art.* New York: Charles Scribner's Sons.

Lippincott, G. (Ed.) (1956). *Dance production.* Washington, D.C.: American Association for Health, Physical Education, and Recreation.

Lockhart, A. (1982). *Modern dance: Building and teaching lessons* (6th ed.). Dubuque, IA: Brown.

McDonagh, D. (1970). *The rise and fall and rise of modern dance.* New York: New American Library.

Melcer, F. (1955). *Staging the dance.* Dubuque, IA: Brown.

Penrod, J., & Plastino, J.G. (1980). *The dancer prepares* (2nd ed.). Palo Alto, CA: Mayfield.

Reid, F. (1982). *The stage lighting handbook* (2nd ed.). New York: Theatre Arts.

Rossman, M., & Bresler, D. (1983). *Guided imagery: An intensive training program for clinicians* (seminar workbook). Pacific Palisades, CA: Institute for Advancement of Human Behavior.

Rugg, H. (1963). *Imagination.* New York: Harper and Row.

Samuels, M.D., & Bennett, H. (1973). *The well body book.* New York: Random House/Bookworks.

Turner, M. (1971). *New dance.* Pittsburgh: University of Pittsburgh Press.

Index

A

motivations for, 18
repetition in, 4-5
parts of, 1
shape or form of, 1, 6-10
style in (*see* Style, dance)
subject of (*see* Subject, of dance)
title of, 18-19
transitions in, 4
unity in, 3
variety in, 4-5
Dance composition. *See also* Blocking; Dance
defined, 103
overall shape of, 1, 12, 109
projection in, 12
Dance dramas, 12, 104
Dance floors
portable, 95, 104
suspended, 94-95, 113
Dance in the round, 61, 104
Dancers
coaching of, 71-72
facial expressions of, 61
groupings of, 63-64, *Figs. 3.11a, 3.11b, and 3.12*
placement of, 49, 58, 59-61
shapes of, 62-63, *Figs. 3.10a, 3.10b, 3.10c, and 3.10d*
Design, 13, 104
Dilley, Barbara, *Fig. 1.1*
Dimmer board, 93, 104. *See also* Lighting
Direction. *See also* Stage directions
defined, 104
manipulation of, 50, *Fig. 3.1*
in phrasing, 2, 3
Downstage
defined, 58, 104
soloist in, *Fig. 4.5c*
use of, 10, 59
Dramatic dance, 8-9
Dress rehearsal, 96, 104
Dressers, 96, 104
Dyeing, of costumes, 80

E

Electronic music, 31, 104

as common dance style, 14
defined, 107
isolations in, 15
pattern of, 15
typical movements of, *Figs. 1.4a and 1.4b*
Jeux (Vivace), 7

K

Kinesthetics
defined, 107
in improvisation, 30, 32
Kuch, Richard, *Fig. 1.3*

L

Lamp, 89, 107
Lamp base, 97, 107
Langer, Suzanne, 70
Lecture-demonstration, 75, 107. *See also* Performance
Legs, of the stage, 85, 88, 107
Leotard. *See also* Costumes; Tights; Unitard
defined, 107
use of, 83-84, *Figs. 4.6b and 4.6c*
Level
defined, 107
of movement, 50, *Fig. 3.2b*
variations in exploration, 28
Lighting
color of, 86, 89-91
of complete stage space, 86-88
cues for, 94
direction of, 86, 88-89
equipment for, 92-93
plot for, 93
pools of, 86-87, *Fig. 4.8*
primary colors of, 89-90
rehearsal for, 93-94
relation to dance, 94
specials, 91-92
Lighting trees, 88, 107
Line
defined, 108
use of, 14

Literal choreography
    defined, 108
    rejection of, 13
    use of, 12
Locomotor, 52, 108
Loose pin hinges, 99, 108, *Fig. 4.12b*
Lyric dance
    in aerobic dance, 21
    as common dance style, 14
    compared to ballet, 15
    defined, 108
    form of, 15
    typical movements in, *Figs. 1.5a, 1.5b, and 1.5c*
Lyric Suite (Minton), 4, 26

M

Manipulation
    in aerobic dance, 53
    in choreography, 49
    of dance energies, 53-55
    defined, 49, 108
    in newer dances, 13
    of shapes, 55, 62-64
    of space, 50-52
    of time, 52-53
Masking, 108
Master tape, 77, 108
McGehee, Helen, *Fig. 1.3*
Meter
    defined, 108
    mixed, 45, 108
    types of, 45
Minton, Sandra, 26
Mirroring
    in dance, 108
    in exploration, 28
Modern dance. *See also* Avant-garde
    defined, 108
    narrative form used in, 8, 12
Monk, Meredith, 67, *Fig. 3.16*
Monotony
    need to avoid, 2

from repetition, 4-5
Motivation
  abstract, 13
  defined, 108
  for improvisation, 36
  simple ideas for, 18
Mounting, 84-86, 109
Music. *See* Accompaniment

N

Narrative form, 8-9, 12, 109
Nikolais Dance Theatre, *Figs. 2.5 and 2.6*
Niven-Cooper, Dale Lee, *Fig. 4.2*
Nonliteral choreography, 13, 109

O

Opposition
  defined, 109
  use of, 65-66, *Figs. 3.14a and 3.14b*
Organic development, 43, 109
Overall shape. *See* Dance composition

P

Pantomime
  defined, 109
  literal movement of, 13
Paths. *See* Pathways
Pathways
  defined, 109
  differences in, 59
Pattern
  of ABA form, 7
  defined, 109
  rhythmic, 37, 111
Paxton, Steve, 67, *Fig. 3.15*
Pedestrian movement, 67, 109
Percussive energy. *See* Energy, percussive
Performance. *See also* Concert; Lecture-demonstration
  accompaniment for, 76-78
  content of, 75-76
  costume changes during, 76

movement away from literal, 13
  selection of, 14, 17
Subject, of dance, 18
Suinn, Richard, 23
Suite, 8, 112
Suite Romance (Campbell), 74
Surrealism, 9, 112
Suspended energy. *See* Energy, suspended
Suspended floor, 94, 113
Sustained energy. *See* Energy, sustained
Swinging, exploration of, 30. *See also* Energy, swinging
Symmetry. *See also* Asymmetry
  of dancers, 63, *Fig. 3.10a*
  defined, 113
  of groupings, 63, *Fig. 3.11a*
Syncopated rhythm
  defined, 113
  of jazz style dance, 15

T

Tactile stimuli, in improvisation, 30, 31, 38
Technical designer, 93, 113
Technical rehearsal, 93-94, 95-96, 113
Technique
  defined, 113
  in improvisation, 32
Tempo
  defined, 113
  manipulation of, 52
  variations in exploration, 28
Tensile Involvement, Fig. 2.5
Tension, blocking due to, 39
Texture
  defined, 113
  in improvisation, 37
Theme
  defined, 113
  stated and manipulated, 7
  and variations, 8, 113
Tights, 83, 114. *See also* Costumes; Leotard
Time
  choreography of, 64-65
  defined, 114